NATIONAL INSTITUTE SOCIAL
SERVICES LIBRARY

Volume 25

MOTHER AND BABY HOMES

MOTHER AND BABY HOMES
A Survey of Homes for Unmarried Mothers

JILL NICHOLSON

LONDON AND NEW YORK

First published in 1968 by George Allen & Unwin Ltd.

This edition first published in 2022
by Routledge
2 Park Square, Milton Park, Abingdon, Oxon OX14 4RN

and by Routledge
605 Third Avenue, New York, NY 10158

Routledge is an imprint of the Taylor & Francis Group, an informa business

© 1968 George Allen & Unwin Ltd.

All rights reserved. No part of this book may be reprinted or reproduced or utilised in any form or by any electronic, mechanical, or other means, now known or hereafter invented, including photocopying and recording, or in any information storage or retrieval system, without permission in writing from the publishers.

Trademark notice: Product or corporate names may be trademarks or registered trademarks, and are used only for identification and explanation without intent to infringe.

British Library Cataloguing in Publication Data
A catalogue record for this book is available from the British Library

ISBN: 978-1-03-203381-5 (Set)
ISBN: 978-1-00-321681-0 (Set) (ebk)
ISBN: 978-1-03-206459-8 (Volume 25) (hbk)
ISBN: 978-1-03-206474-1 (Volume 25) (pbk)
ISBN: 978-1-00-320244-8 (Volume 25) (ebk)

DOI: 10.4324/9781003202448

Publisher's Note
The publisher has gone to great lengths to ensure the quality of this reprint but points out that some imperfections in the original copies may be apparent.

Disclaimer
The publisher has made every effort to trace copyright holders and would welcome correspondence from those they have been unable to trace.

Printed in the United Kingdom
by Henry Ling Limited

MOTHER AND BABY HOMES

A SURVEY OF HOMES FOR UNMARRIED MOTHERS

BY

JILL NICHOLSON

on behalf of the National Council for the Unmarried Mother and her Child

WITH A FOREWORD BY

PROFESSOR LADY WILLIAMS C.B.E.

London
GEORGE ALLEN & UNWIN LTD
RUSKIN HOUSE   MUSEUM STREET

FIRST PUBLISHED IN 1968

This book is copyright under the Berne Convention. Apart from any fair dealing for the purpose of private study, research, criticism or review, as permitted under the Copyright Act, 1956, no portion may be reproduced by any process without written permission. Enquiries should be addressed to the Publishers.

© George Allen and Unwin Ltd, 1968

SBN 04 362 010 8

PRINTED IN GREAT BRITAIN
in 11 on 12pt Fournier type
BY C. TINLING AND CO. LTD
LIVERPOOL, LONDON AND PRESCOT

NATIONAL COUNCIL FOR THE UNMARRIED MOTHER AND HER CHILD
SURVEY OF RESIDENTIAL CARE

Members of the Advisory Committee

Mrs P. E. Voysey (Chairman)	Chairman, N.C.U.M.C. Homes and Hostels Committee
*Sister Gwen Bell	Women's Fellowship of the Methodist Church
Mrs M. E. Bramall, M.A., A.I.M.S.W., J.P.	General Secretary, N.C.U.M.C.
*Miss P. M. Claisse, Ll.B.	Church of England Board for Social Responsibility
†Mr I. J. Croft, M.A.	Home Office Observer
Miss K. E. G. Davidge, M.A., A.I.M.S.W.	Ministry of Health Observer
Dr Rachel A. Elliott, D.PH.	Committee of Management, N.C.U.M.C.
†Rev. Canon P. Harvey	Catholic Child Welfare Council
†Lt.-Colonel Hilda McLauchlan	Salvation Army
†Miss E. M. Magness, B.A.	Church of England Board for Social Responsibility
*Rev. L. T. Munns, Hon. C.F.	Catholic Child Welfare Council
Mrs W. Raphael, B.Sc.	Deputy Chairman, N.C.U.M.C.
*Lt.-Colonel Ada Stevens	Salvation Army
*Lady Stross	Home Office Observer
†Sister Edith Wilding	Women's Fellowship of the Methodist Church

* *Retired*

Sister Gwen Bell	September 1965
Miss P. M. Claisse	November 1964
Rev. L. T. Munns	October 1965
Lt.-Colonel A. Stevens	September 1964
Lady Stross	January 1964

† Joined

July	1965	Mr I. J. Croft in place of Lady Stross
Jan.	1966	Rev. Canon P. Harvey in place of Rev. L. T. Munns
Nov.	1964	Lt.-Colonel H. McLauchlan in place of Lt.-Colonel A. Stevens
Nov.	1964	Miss E. M. Magness in place of Miss Claisse
Sep.	1965	Sister Edith Wilding in place of Sister Gwen Bell

ACKNOWLEDGEMENTS

The project which forms the subject of this book was carried out by a team of three, and I would like to record my personal thanks to Mrs Elizabeth Wilson and Mrs Monica Washburn before we jointly thank all those who helped us.

The research was made possible by grants from the Gullbenkian Foundation and the Ministry of Health. We are grateful to them not only for their financial generosity but for their constant interest throughout the project.

The National Council for the Unmarried Mother and Her Child sponsored the project and undertook the administration associated with it. This was a considerable extra burden for a busy organization and it required co-operation from the staff of all departments. Mrs Margaret Bramall, the General Secretary, was closely associated with all stages of the project. We made heavy demands on her time and patience, and her advice and experience have been invaluable to us. A special word of thanks must also go to the Finance Department and to Mrs J. Woodhouse for work on our behalf.

The research team owes much to the Advisory Committee. We are grateful to the members of the committee for their sustained interest and encouragement, and for their practical assistance. We would also like to thank the organizations which they represented for giving their support to the project, for supplying us with information from their records, and for making it possible for us to visit the Homes for which they were responsible.

Although many people helped us in carrying out the research, without doubt our greatest debts are to Dr Roy Parker and Mr Noel Timms of the London School of Economics. Dr Parker was our research adviser and Mr Timms acted as editorial consultant. This report owes much to their advice and guidance, and we are more than grateful for all the help and encouragement we received from them.

We are most grateful too, to Professor Lady Williams for kindly consenting to write the Foreword to this book.

We also record our thanks to the many other people who gave us assistance and we would particularly like to mention those with whom we were associated for a long period, and who read all or part of the manuscript: Mr Robin Huws Jones, Dr Donald Gough, Sister Dora King, Miss Dorothy Myer and Miss Margaret Yelloly. Our statistical advisers were Mr Alastair Nicholson and Mr Roland Pullen. Others who helped in preparing the report were Mrs Kay Anderson, Mr Roger Garside, Miss Ann Timms, Mrs Veronica Nelson and Mrs Sonia Whittal.

We are very conscious of the debt we owe to all those we interviewed or asked for written information. Matrons, social workers and medical officers of health are busy people, yet they gave up their time and answered our questions willingly. So too did the mothers in the Homes. Although our questioning must have seemed to them just another inquisition, they were anxious to contribute to a study which aimed at providing the information necessary to meet the needs of unmarried mothers more effectively. We hope this report will help to do that, for that would be the justification of the project and the best return to all those who have helped with it.

Finally, again on a personal note, I would like to thank my husband, my mother and my mother-in-law for their generous and uncomplaining help on the domestic front.

FOREWORD

There has recently been much discussion about the plight of the unmarried mother and her child; but very little of it has been based on fact. Many different organizations provide Mother and Baby Homes but as each runs quite independently of the others there has been no means of knowing how far they meet the need. Both the Ministry of Health and the Church of England Board for Social Responsibility have conducted separate studies of Homes, but these were necessarily limited in scope and at a meeting of all the major bodies working to help unmarried mothers a suggestion for a general enquiry was welcomed. The National Council for the Unmarried Mother and Her Child was asked to be responsible and this book is the result. For the first time it is now possible to gain knowledge of the situation as a whole.

Mother and Baby Homes cater each year for between 11,000 and 12,000 of the 70,000 unmarried mothers; but there is hardly one generalization that one can safely make which would be applicable to all the Homes. Some are run by voluntary organizations, some by local authorities, some by religious groups. Some retain the old punitive attitude; others set themselves with much kindness to help the women—many of them very young—to face the difficulties of their position and to plan constructively for their own future and that of their babies.

This book gives the facts but, even more, it gives the feelings and ideas of those most concerned—the mothers-to-be and those who care for them. The chapters which show—mainly in their own words—their hopes and fears, their worries and their preoccupations, are amongst the most valuable.

It is heartening to see—and to hear from the lips of the women themselves—how much of kindness and help they received in these Homes. There are still some who think of Mother and Baby Homes as the old Houses of Correction for Fallen Women. But these, fortunately, are a diminishing minority. Most matrons and committees and their assistants are anxious to do all they can to help their charges through a difficult time.

But, as this book shows, kindness is not enough. Practical problems are dealt with helpfully and sympathetically but there is, as yet, little understanding of the underlying issues and, consequently, little capacity to deal with them. As the concluding chapter argues, what is needed is more flexibility in the use of available provisions as well as the development of other services for those who need a practical alternative to the Homes. But more than anything else it is essential that those who devote themselves with sympathy and kindness to this work should be equipped by proper training to do the even more important job that is needed if these women are to build a happy future for themselves and their children.

Everybody who is concerned about the unmarried mother in residential care should read this book. It offers the first attempt to put the problems in the right context and to offer a constructive method of dealing with them.

Gertrude Williams

CONTENTS

Advisory Committee	page 7
Acknowledgements	9
Foreword	11

CHAPTER

1 INTRODUCTION 17
Development of Residential Care 18
Present Day Context 19
Presentation of the Report 21

2 RESIDENTIAL ACCOMMODATION IN ENGLAND AND WALES 23
Total Provision in 1966 24
Patterns of Administration 26
Role of Local Health Authorities 31

3 THE SURVEY 34
Choosing the Sample 34
Collecting the Material 36

4 THE USE AND SCOPE OF MOTHER AND BABY HOMES 39
Why Mother and Baby Homes are used 39
Mother and Baby Homes as a Method of Care 42
The Framework of the Service offered by the Homes 46

5 THE RESIDENTS IN THE HOMES 51

6 THE MATERIAL STANDARDS 61
General Features 61
Standards of Accommodation 62
Review of Material Standards 65

CONTENTS

7	**THE PATTERN OF DAILY LIFE**	68
	Daily Routine	68
	Food and Meals	69
	Housework	70
	Other Organized Activities	74
	Free Time and Time to go Out	75
8	**RULES**	77
	Concerning Visitors	77
	Other Rules	81
	The Residents' Reactions to the Rules	83
	Enforcing the Rules	84
	Influences on the Rules	85
9	**RELATIONSHIPS IN THE HOMES**	88
	The Residents and the Staff	88
	Relationships amongst the Residents	90
	Influences on Relationships	92
10	**STAFFING**	97
	The Matrons	97
	Other Staff	98
	Qualifications and Staff Establishment	98
	Shortage of Staff	100
	The Staffing Crisis	101
	Sources of Help	103
11	**MEDICAL CARE**	106
	General Medical Care	106
	Ante-natal Care and Preparation for Confinement	107
	Hospital Care	109
	The Place of Confinement	111
12	**THE CARE OF THE BABIES**	115
	Feeding	116
	Bathing	118
	Sleeping Arrangements for the Babies during the Night	118
	Nursery Rules	119
	Review of the 'Mothering Situation'	120

CONTENTS

13	RELIGION IN THE HOMES	123
	Religious Activities in the Voluntary Homes	123
	Views on Spiritual Care	127
	Review of the Religious Purpose of Voluntary Homes	129
14	SOCIAL WORK IN THE HOMES	131
	Arrangements for Social Work in the Homes	131
	Contact between Social Workers and Residents	132
	Relationship between Residents and Social Workers	133
	Need for Social Work Help	134
	Meeting the Need for Casework	139
15	ASSESSMENT AND CONCLUSIONS	141
	Need for Mother and Baby Homes	141
	Adequacy of the Service	142
	Conclusions	147

List of information lodged at the National Council for the Unmarried Mother and Her Child and the National Institute for Social Work Training. 151

Bibliography and List of References 153

1

INTRODUCTION

The subject of this book, residential Homes for unmarried mothers, straddles a number of controversial frontiers. Illegitimate maternity raises questions of sex, morality, religion and authority, parental as as well as communal. The decision each unmarried mother has to face over the future of her baby rouses deep feelings concerning the acceptance or rejection of a continuing mother-child relationship. Because of these issues any service our society provides for unmarried mothers is likely to encounter strong opinion and prejudice. When the service considered is a residential one, further disputed questions are involved. Historically, the provision of residential accommodation for unmarried mothers has been undertaken largely by religious bodies, and even today 138 out of the total of 172 known Homes are provided by church organizations. The religious setting for residential care has been a contentious issue for many years. More recently, the residential method of care itself has been questioned in many fields of social provision.[1] All this makes for a controversial subject of enquiry. Feelings about Mother and Baby Homes run high, convictions, firmly held and fervently asserted, are often based on little evidence or none at all.

We know very little about residential care for unmarried mothers. It was largely to remedy this ignorance and to enable current beliefs and assumptions to be examined that a research project was launched 'to make a critical study of present policies and practices of institutions for the residential care of the unmarried mother and her child in the light of present day needs.'[2] It was intended primarily as a fact finding study to discover what Mother and Baby Homes are like, what they do, and whether the care they offer is appropriate to the needs of those they are trying to help. Part of this information was to come from the residents themselves, who for the first time were to be asked for their

[1] Jones 1966, Townsend 1962.
[2] National Council for the Unmarried Mother and her Child, Memorandum 1963.

views on the care they received. Such a study, it was hoped, would provide the basis for a reassessment of the service in accordance with contemporary needs and modern methods of care.

DEVELOPMENT OF RESIDENTIAL CARE

The forerunners of Mother and Baby Homes appeared around the middle of the eighteenth, and at the beginning of the nineteenth, century. These first residential institutions, known as Penitentiaries or Reformatories, were for the reception of Penitent Prostitutes and their titles mirror the spirit in which they were founded. Though the selective narratives of historians of rescue work may suggest a unity of view which did not in fact exist, looking back to the origins of the work, society was then apparently of one mind towards the unmarried mother. Illegitimacy was a religious and moral problem. Individual sin was the only explanation admitted[1] and personal penitence the only form of atonement. Within such a context the purpose of residential institutions was clear; to reform. Penitents were admitted to these early Homes for periods varying from one to three years. As a condition of entry mothers had to part with their baby,[2] and during their stay, separation from the outside world was absolute, barred windows and locked doors emphasizing the completeness of their isolation. Rigorous religious training and hard work constituted the process of reformation;[3] with intervals for prayer and penitence, inmates spent their days from dawn till dusk in laundry and domestic work, which it was considered would fit them for suitable employment when their atonement was complete.

To modern eyes even the most humane of these reformatories and penitentiaries would seem grim. The image of these early Homes still lingers, and modern Mother and Baby Homes suffer from their past. Yet as institutions they are fundamentally different in character from their predecessors. The long-term training of the old Homes has disappeared, and been replaced by short-term care during the weeks around the confinement. The attitude to the baby has been reversed. Far from requiring a mother to abandon her child, the present Homes almost universally insist that a mother and her baby should spend at least a short time together in the Home. Nor are the Homes as isolated as they were. Some still deliberately restrict the residents' opportunities

[1] Yelloly 1965.
[2] Ferguson and Fitzgerald 1954.
[3] Hall and Howes 1965, Tilley 1966.

for contact with the neighbourhood, but the complete severance of all links between the Homes and the surrounding communities is now unthinkable.

Not only have the Homes themselves changed since the early days of residential care, but the social context in which they operate has altered radically. Much of the confusion and uncertainty surrounding the present service which emerged from the research stems from this fact.

THE PRESENT-DAY CONTEXT

The current attitude to illegitimacy is hard to describe, but certainly it recognizes more than one explanation of the problem. Theories of causation vary from the view that it is no more than an unfortunate consequence of normal behaviour[1] to the psycho-pathological theories advanced by Leontine Young,[2] but whatever view is taken, it is generally admitted now that there is at least some social or emotional content to the problem. The idea of individual sin is no longer dominant.

Along with the lack of certainty as to the basic causes of illegitimacy goes a deep rooted ambivalence in attitudes towards the unmarried mother and the response appropriate to her predicament. On the one hand, unmarried mothers are considered as a group in need of social work support and services designed to help them with the practical and emotional problems of their situation. On the other hand, is an attitude more nearly related to the old idea of sin. This maintains that little should be done to help the unmarried mother; she has brought her difficulties on herself, and some degree of suffering is both appropriate in view of her own conduct, and a deterrent to others. Within this division of opinion, Mother and Baby Homes find themselves criticized for doing both too much and too little.

The clarity of purpose of the early Homes did not survive the abandonment of the sin theory. Religious training ceased to be an acceptable remedy when the social and emotional aspects of the problem were recognized. The irony of this lies in the fact that despite the strong religious emphasis of the early institutions, church organizations seemed to have played no part in their provision;[3] their founders were independent groups of laymen. Yet today when religious training is

[1] Anderson *et al* 1960 cf. also Greenland 1957.
[2] Young 1954.
[3] Hall and Howes 1965.

considered inappropriate, 80 per cent of the Homes are run by official church bodies. This causes concern, for inevitably a religious aura persists in the Church Homes, and fears are sometimes expressed that unmarried mothers are asked 'to pay the price of a pseudo-conversion for the help they receive'.[1]

Although the original purpose of the Homes has gone, no single substitute has taken its place. Nor is there any general agreement outside the Homes on what the functions of a Mother and Baby Home are or should be. During the course of the research we heard them described as shelters, hospitals, boarding houses, reformatories and missionary centres, to list only a few of their ascribed functions. Inevitably this leads to conflicting expectations of the Homes on the part of staff, unmarried mothers, social workers and the general public. Inevitably too, such conflicting expectations give rise to criticism of Mother and Baby Homes. No institution can be expected to fulfil all these functions simultaneously.

In view of this general uncertainty, it is clearly important to identify the actual task of Mother and Baby Homes, and try to see what distinguishes them as a separate class of institution. Their first function, the provision of accommodation for women and girls having an extra-marital pregnancy, is so obvious that it hardly requires a mention. Arising from this, and equally obvious, is the need to provide residents with adequate physical and medical care. There is also a third function, and this deserves more attention. The Homes are expected to provide a service for girls and women whose role as the mother of their child is in doubt. The very great majority of the residents in Mother and Baby Homes are either unsure how long their practical motherhood will last, or else they know definitely that it will be over very shortly. Their situation can be described as one of ambiguous maternity; it is unique and no one knows how to deal with it adequately.

This brings us bluntly to recognize another factor of crucial importance not only for the service of residential care, but for all the other services which may be relevant to the needs of unmarried mothers, including casework, medical services, adoption, fostering, and the daily care of children away from their mothers. We are extremely ignorant about the whole problem of illegitimate maternity. Neither the ultimate causes nor the effects on mother or on child (or we might add, on father who is usually ignored) are well understood. In designing services for unmarried parents and illegitimate children this is a grave handicap. This report is concerned with only one of the available

[1] P. E. P. 1946.

services, and it is one of the smallest. Mother and Baby Homes cater each year for somewhere between 11,000 and 12,000 of the 70,000 women having an extra-marital pregnancy, and they serve them for only three short months out of a pregnancy of nine months and a lifetime of being at least the biological parent of an illegitimate child. The limitations of this study should be recognized if only to focus attention on the wider problems needing investigation.

The context in which present-day Mother and Baby Homes have to work can be summarized in terms of five inter-related themes (i) ignorance of the causes and effects of illegitimate maternity (ii) conflicting social attitudes towards unmarried mothers (iii) confused expectations of Mother and Baby Homes amongst those using them and the general public (iv) the problem of ambiguous maternity and (v) the uncertainty of purpose on the part of those running and staffing the Homes. These five themes are basic to an understanding of the existing situation and they will recur repeatedly throughout the report.

THE PRESENTATION OF THE REPORT

In writing the report we were faced with the problem of what to call the unmarried mothers living in the Homes. It is usual for social workers and residential staff to refer to them as 'girls'. Though we have used this term, it seemed inappropriate for the older women, and in general we have preferred to follow the lead of the Committee of Enquiry into the Staffing of Residential Homes[1] (the Williams Committee) and refer to those being cared for as 'residents'. It will be seen, however, that even this term is not entirely appropriate.

The next two chapters establish the framework for the rest of the report. The first sets out the total provision of residential accommodation for unmarried mothers in England and Wales. The second describes the sample of Homes visited and the methods used in the survey. Then follows the main section of the report presenting the material collected during the survey. This is based on the evidence of those interviewed supplemented by our own observations during the interviews and the visits to the Homes. To let the reader share the impressions we ourselves received, we have in many cases allowed those interviewed to speak for themselves, quoting their own words wherever possible. This part of the report opens with a discussion of the use made of residential accommodation and a description of the residents interviewed. Following these are five chapters concerned with the

[1] *Caring for People*, Williams Report, 1967.

subjects common to any residential institution; the material standards, the pattern of daily life, the rules, the relationships in the Home and the staffing situation. Then four chapters deal with aspects of care particular to Mother and Baby Homes; medical care, the care of the babies, religion and social work. It is in these four chapters that the relevance of the five themes mentioned is most obvious. In a final chapter, the Homes visited are assessed and from the evidence produced by the survey some general conclusions regarding the developments of the service are considered.

2

RESIDENTIAL ACCOMMODATION IN ENGLAND AND WALES

This enquiry, like other recent studies of residential care[1] faced two initial problems. The first was to choose an appropriate definition of the accommodation to be studied. Mother and Baby Homes are provided especially for women and girls who need accommodation by reason of an extra-marital pregnancy. There are Homes which do just this, but others merge imperceptibly into 'shelters' or 'hostels' for anyone in need of temporary accommodation, or into private households which continually have a number of unmarried mothers living in the family home. For the purpose of the research, Mother and Baby Homes were considered to be institutions whose main function was to provide accommodation for women and girls having an extra-marital pregnancy. As a working definition this was adequate, but the divisions between the different types of institution are not too sharp.

The second problem was to compile a comprehensive list of all the Homes to which this definition applied. There is no central list of known Homes, and no legal requirements for registration which cover all the Homes within the scope of the study. There are, however, a number of directories and handbooks published by organizations providing Mother and Baby Homes giving details of their own Homes, and those run by bodies associated with them. From these, a Directory of Homes and Hostels being prepared by the National Council for the Unmarried Mother and her Child, and a list of Homes known to the Ministry of Health, we compiled our own register. A further difficulty is that published directories rapidly become out of date. We had to supplement our original sources of information by enquiries through social workers and by following up reports of Homes appearing in the press. By April 1964, 169 Homes had been listed and these were used as the basis for planning the sample survey. At a later stage, we were granted permission by the Ministry of Health to check this list against

[1] Townsend 1962, *Caring for People*, Williams Report, 1967.

the returns made by local health authorities in respect of Mother and Baby Homes for 1964. Each authority is required by the Ministry to make a yearly return for every Mother and Baby Home within its area. The returns yielded a total of only 144 Homes. Amongst those missing were Homes which to our knowledge were either in receipt of grant aid from their authority or registered by their authority as a Nursing Home. During the course of the survey there were repeated changes both in the number and the type of Homes on our original list and this was constantly amended as new information became available. This chapter describes the provision of residential accommodation in England and Wales in 1966 when there were 172 Homes on our register.

TOTAL PROVISION IN 1966

Types of Accommodation

Residential accommodation for unmarried mothers falls into three categories—accommodation in the early months of pregnancy; accommodation around the period of confinement; and accommodation for unmarried mothers who keep their children. The second category is by far the largest, and for reasons explained in the next chapter, this category alone forms the subject of the rest of the report. Here, however, the full provision is described. Some homes offer more than one type of accommodation, for example Homes which normally cater for the confinement period may take in girls in early pregnancy and let them go out to work, or the mothers who keep their children may continue to live in the Home for a time, working either in the Home or the neighbourhood. Some Homes offer these forms of care as a matter of policy, others do so exceptionally in response to particular circumstances. For the purposes of the research, Homes were classified according to their main function.

1. Accommodation for Pregnant Girls

There are twelve Homes for pregnant girls each run on hostel lines. Most have shared bedrooms and communal living rooms, though one has single self-contained bed-sitting rooms with their own kitchenette. There is no definite period of stay in these hostels. Residents come in fairly early in pregnancy and stay until a few weeks before their expected date of confinement when they will probably transfer to a Home catering for the confinement period. While in the hostel residents generally go out to work and contribute part of their earnings towards the fees of the Home. If they cannot find work they may have to rely on Social Security payments.

2. Accommodation around the Confinement Period

154 Mother and Baby Homes cater for the weeks around the confinement period. Thirty-two of the Homes have their own Maternity unit and all normal deliveries take place in these Homes. The residents in the other Homes, which we have called 'Before and After Care Homes', are admitted to local maternity hospitals for their confinement. Homes of both types usually admit residents about six weeks before the expected date of confinement and expect them to stay until the baby is about six weeks old. The exact length of stay varies from Home to Home. So too does the rigidity with which the formal ruling operates. A number of Homes allow the length of stay to be adapted to individual circumstances particularly after the baby's birth, and a recent survey carried out by the Moral Welfare Workers Association found far more variation in length of stay than is generally supposed.[1] Amongst the Homes in this category are four which provide special facilities. Three cater for very young girls still receiving full-time education, providing daily schooling and special coaching for public examinations. The fourth Home, which also provides schooling, is a training Home for young girls in need of care and protection or on probation. In these four Homes there is no fixed length of stay.

3. Accommodation for Mothers with Children

Accommodation in this category may be of two kinds. Some Homes, in general the older ones, are run on the hostel principle, with supervisory staff and at least some facilities for communal use. In others the intention is to give the residents as far as possible their own private family home. In this case the accommodation takes the form of self-contained flatlets or bed-sitting rooms, and the relationship between the residents and the organizers of the Home is similar to that between tenants and their landlord. In projects of this kind, supervision is kept to a minimum, though there may be a warden or a married couple living in one of the flatlets who keep a friendly eye on their co-tenants. In either type of Home the mothers usually go out to work and the babies are cared for in a nursery attached to the Home or in a nearby day-nursery. Some Homes limit the time for which accommodation is available; two years is perhaps the most common period. In others there is no definite time-limit though residents are encouraged to put their name on the local authority housing list.

It was in this category of accommodation that the changes in total provision throughout the survey period were most marked. Our

[1] *Bulletin* 1966.

initial list contained four Homes for mothers and children, all run on the hostel principle. Another hostel and a set of flatlets had been added when the tables for this chapter were compiled. Since then, however, the growth in accommodation of the flatlet and bed-sitting room type has been dramatic. Twelve projects are known to have opened recently and others are being planned. Many of these are designed for all groups of unsupported mothers, widows and divorced or separated wives as well as unmarried mothers. They are, therefore, strictly outside the terms of reference for this research project but they should at least be mentioned here as a new and apparently popular form of accommodation.

Size of Homes
The Williams Committee found that Mother and Baby Homes are small in comparison with other types of residential institutions. The average Home for Unmarried Mothers has thirteen residents, Old People's Homes have forty-six, Nurseries for children under five have twenty-three, and only Hostels for working boys and girls with an average of twelve residents were smaller than the Homes we were studying. Table 1 shows the size of the different types of Homes for unmarried mothers. It can be seen that Homes with their own Maternity Units tend to be large.

Organizations providing Mother and Baby Homes
Mother and Baby Homes may be provided by voluntary or statutory bodies. The bulk of the provision is made by voluntary organizations associated with the different churches. Three kinds of statutory authority have power to provide accommodation: the Health, Welfare and the Children's Departments of County Councils, County Borough Councils and London Borough Councils. The part played by different organizations in the provision of Mother and Baby Homes is shown in the two following tables. Table 2 shows the number and type of Homes run by different organizations, and Table 3 the number of beds in each type of Home provided by the different organizations.

PATTERNS OF ADMINISTRATION

The administrative pattern of residential care is extremely complicated, and as early as 1946 gave rise to the view that 'Overall co-ordination (of the services) on a regional or even national level is essential.'[1]

[1] P. E. P. 1946.

Table 1

Size of Homes by different types of accommodation (1966)

Type of Home	1–5	6–10	11–15	16–20	21–25	26–30	Over 30	Totals	%
Accommodation for pregnant girls	—	4	5	3	—	—	—	12	7.0
Accommodation around confinement period:									
1. Maternity Homes	—	1	4	8	11	4	4	32	18.6
2. Before and After Care Homes	3	27	43	28	12	6	3	122	70.9
Accommodation for mothers who keep their children	2	2	—	—	1	1	—	6	3.5
TOTALS	5 (2.9%)	34 (19.7%)	52 (30.2%)	39 (22.7%)	24 (14.0%)	11 (6.4%)	7 (4.1%)	172	(100.0%)

Table 2

Types of Homes provided by various organizations (1966)

	Number of Homes					
	Around confinement period					
Organization	For pregnant girls	Maternity Homes	Before and After-Care Homes	For Mothers who keep their children	Totals	%
Voluntary bodies						
Religious Organizations:						
Church of England	7	10	80	3	100	58.0
Roman Catholic	3	8	9	—	20	11.6
Salvation Army	—	7	2	—	9	5.3
Methodist Church	2	1	2	1	6	3.5
Other Churches	—	2	1	—	3	1.8
Other	—	4	5	1	10	5.8
Statutory Bodies						
Local Authorities (Health, Welfare Departments)[1]	—	—	23	1	24	14.0
TOTALS	12 (7.0%)	32 (18.6%)	122 (70.9%)	6 (3.5%)	172	100

[1] There were no Homes run by Childrens' Departments when the statistics for this table were compiled. See p. 30.

Table 3
Beds in Homes provided by various organizations (1966)

Organization	For pregnant girls	Around confinement period — Maternity Homes	Around confinement period — Before and After-Care Homes	For Mothers who keep their children	Totals	%
Voluntary bodies						
Religious Organizations:						
Church of England	83	179	1080	31	1373	47.6
Roman Catholic	38	298	228	—	564	19.6
Salvation Army	—	150	41	—	191	6.6
Methodist Church	31	22	24	10	87	3.0
Other Churches	—	49	8	—	57	2.0
Other	—	68	73	10	151	5.2
Statutory bodies						
Local Authorities (Health, Welfare Departments)[1]	—	—	433	28	461	16.0
Totals	152 (5.3%)	766 (26.6%)	1887 (65.4%)	79 (2.7%)	2884	100

[1] See footnote Table 2

On the voluntary side, there are four major organizations and more than three times as many smaller ones, all operating on a different basis. Only one of the major organizations, the Salvation Army, provides a national service; the work of its nine Homes in England and Wales is co-ordinated and controlled directly by the Headquarters of the Women's Social Work. Two of the Homes provided by Methodists are also run by a national organization—the Women's Fellowship of the Methodist Church, but the other four are the responsibility of local missions centred on local Churches. Both Anglican and Roman Catholic Homes operate within the Diocesan framework of their church administration. Each of the forty-nine Anglican dioceses in England and Wales, and each of the twenty Roman Catholic dioceses is solely responsible for its own social work. Individual Homes within a diocese are rarely if ever run according to a common code of practice; and there is not necessarily even any co-ordination between the facilities they offer. Church of England Homes are likely to be affiliated more or less formally to the diocesan organization, but control of each Home is still firmly in the hands of its own management committee which retains complete authority over organization and policy. The management committee may be a committee or sub-committee of the diocesan or deanery organization, but it may also be independent and have no place in the structure of church administration. An even more marked autonomy exists in Roman Catholic Mother and Baby Homes. Homes are provided by religious orders and by bodies of lay Catholics. These bodies will probably have strong ties with the diocesan organization and its social workers, but they are unlikely to form a structural part of the administrative system.

On the statutory side different acts empower each of the three departments of local government to make similar provision. Local health authorities may provide services for unmarried mothers as part of the general duty laid on them by the National Health Service Act, 1946, to care for all expectant and nursing mothers and young children. Welfare departments may act, as they do in the London boroughs, under powers conferred by Part III of the National Assistance Act 1945 to provide for persons in need of temporary accommodation. The Children Act 1948 and the Children and Young Persons Act 1963 gave wide permissive powers to local authority children's departments, making possible a broad range of services. Until recently, these powers were not used to provide Mother and Baby Homes, but now two children's departments run Homes, both of which have opened since the statistics for this chapter were compiled.

ROLE OF LOCAL HEALTH AUTHORITIES

In practice, the local health authorities are the most active of the statutory authorities in providing for unmarried mothers. They are empowered both to provide services directly, and to assist and supervise those run by voluntary bodies. Local authorities generally prefer the second method of provision. By this they give financial assistance to voluntary Homes. They may also require the Homes within their area to be registered and inspected by the authority. The information necessary to describe the policies and practices of local health authorities on a national basis was not available so a special enquiry was undertaken in the regions we decided (see chapter 3) to survey. The activities of local health authorities as they affected the voluntary Homes we studied are described briefly below. More detailed information is available from the National Council for the Unmarried Mother and her Child and the National Institute for Social Work Training.

Local Health Authority financial assistance to voluntary Homes
Local health authority financial assistance to voluntary Homes may be made either as an annual block grant, or as separate *per capita* grants for individual residents.

Block Grants: Ten of the nineteen voluntary Homes in the survey region received annual grants from their own local authority, and three Homes were allocated block grants by neighbouring authorities whose unmarried mothers used the Homes. Seven of the Homes received sums ranging from £200 to £1100. These grants were intended to cover the difference between the cost to the Home of maintaining residents from the granting authority's area, and the proportion of the fees the residents paid directly to the Home. Even if the sum granted was not sufficient to meet this gap, and two matrons reported that it was not, the authorities did not subsidize the fees of individual residents on a per capita basis. Five Homes received small annual grants ranging from £70 to £445, and in these cases the local health authorities usually also paid *per capita* grants when their cases used the Homes.

None of the authorities giving block grants reserved beds in the Home for their own use, or tied the amount of the grant to the numbers of mothers admitted from their area, but four Homes were expected to give priority to applications from local unmarried mothers. Sometimes other conditions were laid on the acceptance of grants: four Homes had to be open to local health authority inspection, and five accepted the right of the local health authority to nominate members of the Homes' management committee.

Per Capita Grants: Local authorities not making block grants to a Home usually subsidize residents' fees on a *per capita* basis. Each authority determines its own particular method for doing this, and some were much more generous than others. Voluntary Homes admit residents from many different local authority areas, including those outside the survey regions. The great variety of practice amongst local authorities meant that residents in similar circumstances sometimes received widely differing amounts of aid. First the authorities varied in the conditions under which they would grant aid. Generally it appeared that the need for accommodation alone was sufficient qualification for a grant, but in some authorities certain conditions such as an applicant's age, the length of time she had lived in the area, the number of previous pregnancies, or even the particular Home she wished to go to, might determine her eligibility for assistance. The authorities varied too in the proportion of the fees they would pay, and on the basis on which this was assessed. Most authorities determined the size of their contribution after considering how much the applicant herself could pay from National Insurance benefits and allowances from the National Assistance Board as it then was. Others, however, considered every possible source of income before fixing their grant, and expected that all or part of the maternity grant and dependents' allowance would be paid over to the Homes. Some authorities hoped that the resident's parents or the putative father would make some contribution towards the fees of the Mother and Baby Home. Some stipulated that every effort should be made to collect money from these sources irrespective of the fact that parents have no legal obligation to maintain their daughter after the age of sixteen, and that a putative father's agreement to contribute towards the fees of a Mother and Baby Home could be construed as admission of paternity in the event of affiliation proceedings. A third source of variation was the length of time for which authorities were prepared to give help. A fairly normal period was thirteen weeks, but it might be more, or it might be less. Sometimes the specified number of weeks included the period spent in hospital; sometimes it did not. Some authorities could be relied upon to continue their contributions beyond the normal limit of time if the baby was late, or if the future of mother and child had not been settled. Some would only do this in very special circumstances, and some not at all.

Registration and Inspection of Voluntary Homes

The Acts affecting the registration of voluntary Mother and Baby Homes are the Public Health Act 1936 and the Nursing Homes Act 1963. The first gave local health authorities the power to register voluntary Maternity Homes. The second repealed a clause of the earlier Act which had allowed certain categories of voluntary Homes to be exempt from registration. Since the 1963 Act all Maternity Homes have to be registered, but in respect of Before and After-Care Homes the legislation is open to different interpretations, and it is still a matter for each local authority to decide whether or not to register the Before and After-Care Homes in its area. Five of those in the survey regions were registered.

The ten Homes in the survey areas (five Maternity Homes and five Before and After-Care Homes) registered under the Public Health Act 1936 were required to comply with the standards laid down in the Act and to be open to inspection by officers of the local health authority or the Ministry of Health. In addition to these, five non-registered Homes were also regularly inspected by the local health authority. Only four voluntary Homes, two in each region, were not inspected. Of the two in the North, one was said by the medical officer of health to be under constant supervision by his department, and the other had a good informal relationship with the authority.

3

THE SURVEY

CHOOSING THE SAMPLE

We wanted to visit a sample of Homes which would be reasonably representative of the national provision taking into account both the organizations providing Homes and the type of accommodation they offered. We also wanted to study the range of facilities available within a given area. For this reason a random sample of Homes covering the whole country was inappropriate, and it was decided to concentrate the study on two of the Registrar General's Standard Regions of England and Wales, and to visit all the Homes within them. One region in the north of England was chosen and one in the south. Between them they covered industrial, rural and urban areas, and they included twenty-six Mother and Baby Homes—15 per cent of the total known provision. Fifteen were in the northern region, and eleven in the southern. Table 4 shows the twenty-six Homes in the survey areas classified by organization and type of accommodation.

Table 4 shows the Homes in the survey areas as they were when the study was designed in April 1964. Between then and January 1965, when the visits began, there were several changes. First we learnt of the existence of a small Home of the flatlet type for mothers with children; the chairman of the committee organizing this Home was interviewed, but because the intention of the project was to give the mothers a private home of their own to which the only visitors would be those invited by the mothers themselves, it was not possible to include this Home in the survey. Next, two Maternity Homes closed, and another which offered accommodation around the period of confinement moved and re-opened in the region as a special Home for schoolgirls. Finally, the only Home offering accommodation in the early months of pregnancy closed. This meant that the twenty-three Homes visited consisted solely of those catering for the period around the confinement.

Table 4
Homes in the Survey Areas by Organization and type of Accommodation (1964)

	For pregnant girls	Around confinement period Maternity Homes	Before and After-Care Homes	For Mothers with children	Total
Voluntary bodies					
Church of England Organizations	1	3	13	—	17
Other religious organizations	—	4	1	—	5
Other	—	—	—	—	0
Statutory bodies					
Local health authorities[1]	—	—	4	—	4
TOTAL	1	7	18	0	26

[1] The only Homes provided by welfare departments are in the London boroughs and the survey regions did not include the London area.

COLLECTING THE MATERIAL

The survey had two objects: to build up a picture of the residential care available, and to study how far the provision met the needs of unmarried mothers in the survey regions. To achieve the first object, we visited every Home within the two regions, and interviewed the matron and the residents. During the visit we made a tour of the building and took notes of the number and function of the rooms, the equipment and the standard of furniture, furnishings and decoration. To assist our assessment of how far the need for residential care was being answered, we interviewed fifty-one social workers in the regions. Unmarried mothers almost always make a booking for a Mother and Baby Home through the social worker who has been helping them through their pregnancy. We wished to examine the way in which social workers used the Homes for their clients, and to obtain their judgement on the adequacy of the range of facilities in the regions, and the quality of the individual Homes. Of the social workers interviewed, twenty-five were Church of England moral welfare workers, nine were Roman Catholic welfare workers or priests working full time in the field, nine were children's or child care officers, six were welfare workers employed to assist unmarried mothers by local health authorities and two were Methodist welfare workers. Both the Methodist welfare workers work from London, but their help is available to unmarried mothers all over the country.

The unmarried mothers in the Homes were interviewed in small groups, usually numbering between four and eight. The population of the Homes was defined as the number of unmarried mothers resident or in hospital on the first day of the visit, and the total sample yielded 296 residents: 185 in the north and 111 in the south. Altogether 250 residents (including an additional three who were admitted to the Home after the first day of the visit) were interviewed; 151 in the north and ninety-nine in the south. Of the 49 residents who were not interviewed, 30 were in hospital or in bed in the Mother and Baby Home, 9 were in the one Home where the matron selected the residents to be interviewed, 5 were unwilling to be interviewed and 1 was at work. There was no information on why the other 4 residents did not attend an interview.

Group interviewing as a research technique is not widely used, but it proved in this case to be most successful. Discussions were lively and covered a variety of subjects revealing strong views and a wide range of opinions. During the course of the survey it became obvious that the residents of Mother and Baby Homes gain a great measure of comfort and support simply from being together, and in the interviews a strong sense of group unity was often apparent. Discussions often touched on personal difficulties and sometimes individual problems were raised not by the individual concerned, but by another member of the group. Apart from the factual information produced by the group interviews, the nature of the discussions themselves was also informative. From their manner of speaking it was often possible to gain an insight into the relationship of different members of the group with one another, and also into the relationship between the residents and the staff. At the end of the group interviews, each member of the group was asked to complete a questionnaire. The response to this was excellent. Although there were more than fifty questions, and it took on average more than half an hour to complete, the response rate to individual questions rarely fell below 80 per cent and it was usually much higher. 240 residents completed the questionnaire. Seven had to leave the interview before the schedules were handed out, and three were unwilling to fill them in.

We also interviewed individually the most recently arrived resident and the mother who was next to leave the Home. The subject of both group and individual interviews was intended to be the same; the life of the Mother and Baby Home and the residents' attitude towards it. By contrast with the groups, however, the individual interviews were less successful. When residents were seen on their own, it was difficult to persuade them to talk about the Home. They wanted to tell us about themselves, the problems they faced in planning for the baby, how their parents had reacted to their pregnancy and what their boy friend felt about the situation. This was true whether or not the individual had previously taken part in a group interview. Interesting though such information was, it was not the focus of the study, and relatively little use of this material has been made in the report.

In all the interviews a combination of scheduled questions and informal discussion was used. For the interviews with matrons, residents, and social workers separate lists of topics were prepared. Copies of these and the schedules used may be obtained from the National Council for the Unmarried Mother and her Child and the National Institute for Social Work Training. The list of topics for discussion set the broad framework of the interviews but within this, the order in which individual topics were raised, their relative importance and the time spent discussing each one were left to those being interviewed. Only a minimum number of notes was taken during the interviews. As soon as possible afterwards, each interview was recorded on tape according to a standard set of detailed headings.

This form of guided discussion was chosen as the most appropriate method to use in covering a wide area of unchartered ground. Inevitably, however, quantifying the data produced was difficult. Sometimes information on a particular point of detail was lacking because the topic had not arisen in the discussion, and we faced further problems when different sources of information in the same Home produced conflicting evidence. Because of these difficulties the numbers given throughout the report, other than those based on the questionnaires, should be treated with caution. They may fairly be taken as a guide to relative proportions, but they should not be regarded as definitive.

4

THE USE AND SCOPE OF MOTHER AND BABY HOMES

In considering how Mother and Baby Homes are used, two initial points should be made. In the first place, they represent only one of the services potentially available to the unmarried mother who needs help around the confinement period. Social Security benefits can assist her in retaining her independence while she is not working. Families who take unmarried pregnant girls on an *au-pair* or paying-guest basis provide an alternative to living alone in lodgings or a bed-sitter for those who cannot stay at home until the baby is born. And afterwards, if a mother cannot or does not wish to care for her baby, the child can be fostered or placed in a nursery pending an adoption placement. We wished to find out why some unmarried mothers need the particular service of a Mother and Baby Home. The first part of the chapter deals with this question, and discusses how social workers use the available range of residential Homes to meet the individual needs of their clients. The second point is that Mother and Baby Homes are not generally open to any unmarried mother simply on the grounds of need. All the Homes visited employed certain admission criteria and most also stipulated the period for which accommodation was available. The use that can be made of the service is, therefore, partly determined by the Homes themselves, and the conditions they impose are discussed in the second part of the chapter.

WHY MOTHER AND BABY HOMES ARE USED

In a sense it is the social workers rather than the residents who are more correctly described as the 'users' of Mother and Baby Homes. The social worker to whom the unmarried mother goes for help knows the whole range of potential services available, suggests residential accommodation if it seems appropriate and eventually selects and arranges the booking of a Mother and Baby Home if a client needs this. Only 8 of the 240 girls who answered our questionnaire had made their own arrangements to go into a Mother and Baby Home. Apart from 5 girls who gave no information, all other bookings had been made by the social workers who had been helping the residents through their pregnancy. We asked both the social workers and the residents why unmarried mothers go into Mother and Baby Homes. Though the answers given by both groups were similar, there were sufficient differences to make it worthwhile presenting them separately.

The Social Workers' Reasons

The unmarried mothers who go into Mother and Baby Homes form only a small proportion of their social workers' case load,[1] and it would seem that they are a distinct group, largely because they include such a high percentage of those who intend to have their baby adopted. A few clients who are undecided about the baby's future may go into a Home, but those who plan to keep their child go into a Home only if for some special reason they cannot stay in their own home.

One of the reasons most commonly given for admission to a Mother and Baby Home was the lack of alternative services. Many social workers reported that foster homes and nursery places were almost impossible to find, so that a client who did not want to take her baby home had little choice but to go into a Mother and Baby Home. Another common reason was fear of social ostracism, and this was also found in the survey undertaken by the Moral Welfare Workers Association.[2] Many social workers reported that parents sometimes feared social disgrace more strongly than their daughter and this aroused considerable tension in the family. Sometimes too existing family tensions were aggravated by the pregnancy, and social workers saw both situations as accounting for some admissions to Mother and Baby Homes. The last of the major reasons for admission was accommodation problems. These included those who were homeless and the few cases in which girls were turned out by their parents. In addition there were some clients who would have stayed at home but for practical difficulties; their mother was ill, or out at work, or there was

---

[1] It has been impossible to give any precise estimate of the proportion. Statistics of unmarried mothers consulting a social worker and those admitted to Mother and Baby Homes were only available from the Church of England Committee for Diocesan Moral and Social Welfare Councils and the Roman Catholic Crusade of Rescue. Based on figures for 1965 about one-fifth of those consulting a Church of England Moral Welfare Worker were admitted to a Mother and Baby Home. The proportion for the Roman Catholics was two-thirds. In both cases the national figures conceal wide variations in statistics from different areas.

[2] *Bulletin* 1966.

simply no room in the house for a baby. Other reasons were less common. Four social workers mentioned that parents sometimes arranged for their daughters to go into a Mother and Baby Home in an attempt to break up a relationship with the putative father. Three said that the shortage of hospital beds accounted for some admissions. Sometimes the only way to ensure adequate arrangements for the confinement was to book a place for a client in a Maternity Home or a Before and After-Care Home which had a special allocation of hospital beds.

The Residents' Reasons

As far as the residents were concerned the overwhelming reason for coming into a Mother and Baby Home was adoption; if they had been going to keep their baby they would have stayed at home in the normal way. There was a prevalent impression amongst the residents that going into a Mother and Baby Home provided 'the best', 'the quickest' or even 'the only way' of getting the baby adopted. There were also many residents who had initially imagined that 'the baby would be adopted straight from hospital' and that they could go home. In fact placement from hospital is rarely practicable, and once the residents had understood that the legal process of adoption could not begin until the baby was six weeks old, they themselves saw no option to going into a Mother and Baby Home; how else would they care for the baby? Complete ignorance of other services such as fostering or nursery care was widespread, and it was clear that there were mothers in the Homes who would not have been there had they known about and been able to arrange alternative means of caring for the baby pending the adoption placement. Next, and particularly common in the south, came the wish to get away from the neighbours. We found in our discussions with the residents that few succeeded in keeping their pregnancy secret. Many intended to do so but about three-quarters of them said that the neighbours ultimately found out. Even so, it was a relief to get away from the gossip and avoid the embarrassment they felt because 'everybody was nosey and also stared'. Quite often it seemed the residents might have been prepared to withstand public disapproval for themselves; they left home to protect their families. Typical of these was a girl who said 'my parents are very well known business people in my home town and if I stayed there it would be most unpleasant for my family and myself'. In this connection several girls mentioned younger brothers and sisters; it would be 'unfair to them if I was at home as people do talk and are spiteful to the whole family'. The list of accommodation problems mentioned by the residents was similar to that given by the social workers. The practical difficulties of remaining in their own home were more common amongst the residents of the northern Homes than those in the south. Then there were those who were literally homeless. Seventeen stated specifically on their questionnaire that this was so, and in seven other cases it seemed likely from the answers given that they were also homeless. These numbers included all the foreign girls, most of those from Ireland, and several whose families were abroad. Only six of the residents we saw said that they had been turned out of the house, and that one or other parent (usually their father) 'would not have me at home owing to the fact that they didn't want anyone to know'.

Finally, there were two reasons given by the residents which were not mentioned by the social workers. First, the wish of some to be alone when working out the decision about the baby. This attitude was particularly prevalent in one or two northern Homes where the residents had made no secret of their condition, and where they continued to visit their parents and friends almost daily while they were in the Home. To them, admission to a Mother and Baby Home was a chance 'to get away from people I know and a valuable opportunity to think about life and to study the advantages of keeping the baby and the disadvantages. I think that this time is needed because you must be sure what you really want for the baby'. Secondly, six residents claimed that they were in the Mother and Baby Home because they had been 'talked into it' or just 'sent' by their social worker. One of these said there had been no discussion about going into a Home. Her social worker had simply handed her a piece of paper saying 'sign this', and then told her 'now you're going to... Mother and Baby Home'. Two others who could and would have stayed at home did not realize that they were free to do so. One explained on her questionnaire, 'as far as I can remember, my mother and I weren't actually given a choice, or if it comes to that, we didn't realize whether there was a choice or not'. And for all the other girl knew, 'it was the law or something'.

MOTHER AND BABY HOMES AS A METHOD OF CARE

These were the reasons which social workers and residents gave for unmarried mothers going into Mother and Baby Homes. We also discussed with the social workers the use of residential Homes as a means of care. Here the confused image of Mother and Baby Homes, and the lack of agreement on their purpose was evident. Nearly all the social workers agreed that accommodation in a Mother and Baby Home was particularly suitable for certain cases, and that they would encourage certain of their clients to go into a Home rather than use other available facilities.

There was, however, no agreement on the kind of case for which Mother and Baby Homes were particularly suitable. According to different social workers such cases were variously defined as those with tension in the family, pregnant girls living alone, those who were uncertain of the baby's future, 'the more refined girls', the 'working class girls' and the 'girls of easy virtue'. In contrast to the general view, three social workers said they encouraged clients who were keeping their baby to go into a Home, particularly if they would have to return to work afterwards, because it gave them some time on their own to get to know and love the child. Six workers liked most of their clients to go to a Mother and Baby Home whatever their problems or circumstances.

Similarly there was no agreement on what residential care was supposed to achieve. To the workers who saw the aim of Mother and Baby Homes as 'the salvation of souls', residential care offered valuable spiritual and moral guidance; a stay in a Home could 'put girls back on the right path'. Alternatively, the Homes might be regarded as a means of enabling the girls to experience motherhood, and of bringing home to them their responsibilities for the child. Different again was the view of residential care as a setting in which a client could be helped to gain a sense of perspective about her situation and to realize that she was not the only one to face an illegitimate pregnancy. Objectives of reform, accommodation and care were all apparent in the different ways the Homes were used. It is hardly surprising that matrons complained that residents were sometimes sent to them who were unsuited to the life of a Mother and Baby Home and who had no need of the care they offered. This lends support to the findings of another survey that 'hard-pressed out-door workers[1] were sometimes tempted to regard admission to a Mother and Baby Home as the obvious answer to the girl's predicament without perhaps giving sufficient consideration to possible alternatives'.[2]

---

[1] 'Out-door workers' is the term often used to distinguish those social workers employed by the Church of England who work in the community from those employed in residential work. See also page 98.
[2] Hall and Howes 1965.

Selecting a Home

Whatever their purpose in using residential care, social workers take considerable trouble to select a particular home for each client. The client's age, her background and personality are all taken into account in choosing a Home where she will make a good relationship with the matron and fit in easily with the other residents. At least that was the aim, but social workers often found in practice that freedom of choice was hampered by factors over which they had little control.

The most frustrating of these, from the casework point of view, was the policy of some local health authorities in assisting unmarried mothers in need of residential care. Authorities which run Mother and Baby Homes of their own or subsidize a local voluntary Home expect unmarried mothers from their area to use these Homes, and do not willingly make grants towards the fees of Homes outside the area. In this situation, a social worker has no option but to use a particular Home however unsuitable she may consider it. This restriction affected the Roman Catholic moral welfare workers less than their colleagues from other organizations as local authorities usually made exceptions so that girls could attend Homes of their own denomination.

The geographical distribution of Homes limited the choice of social workers who had few Homes in their area. This problem occurred more often in the south than in the north. At least some clients needing accommodation had to be sent to Homes a good distance away, where visits from the social worker and from the girl's own family were necessarily infrequent. The social workers did not ordinarily refer their cases to a local social worker but placed their more mature and self-reliant girls in the distant Homes and reserved the nearer ones for the cases that needed more support.

Then there were cases which were difficult to place because the rules of so many Homes excluded them. Amongst these were the girls who had already had an illegitimate baby, the married women, the so-called 'prostitute type', the girls with a history of delinquency, and the physically handicapped. It was suggested that special Homes were needed to cater for these last two categories. It was also virtually impossible to make any careful choice of Home for the clients who only contacted a welfare worker towards the end of their pregnancy; 14 per cent of the girls we saw made their first contact with a welfare worker in the last three months. All that could be done for them was to try to find a Home with a vacancy.

Finally, if a worker is really going to match her clients to the Homes, she must have a good knowledge of both. This condition was not always fulfilled. The moral welfare workers who had to use Homes a long way from their office admitted that they knew little about them, and child care officers who rarely used Mother and Baby Homes simply looked in the Directory published by the National Council for the Unmarried Mother and her Child to find the nearest one. The social worker's knowledge of her clients clearly depends on the number of times she was able to see them before arranging for them to go to a Mother and Baby Home. Only one social worker was able to describe a definite pattern of interviews during this period. She saw new clients about once a week for three weeks, then once a fortnight for the next month or so, and then weekly again until the client went into the Home. One moral welfare worker tried to see all her cases once a month. None of the others were as specific as this: they saw clients 'once or twice', or 'a few times', and social workers in towns tended to see their clients more often than those who had to travel over a large country district. Exactly how often a social worker saw a client depended on a set of circumstances including the severity of the girl's problems, and this perhaps explains why we found no relationship between the number of interviews and the stage of pregnancy at which a client first contacted a social worker.

More than three-quarters of the residents had in fact first contacted a social worker during the first six months of pregnancy; 31 per cent during the first three months, and 49 per cent between four and six months; as we have seen only 14 per cent left it until the last three months (and 6 per cent gave no information). To assess the opportunity a worker would have to get to know her client before placing her in a Mother and Baby Home, we counted the meetings each resident had with her social worker during this period. In doing this we separated from the 227 residents known to have been in touch with a social worker those (66) who had seen more than one worker as we did not know which of the workers seen had been responsible for the placement. The remaining 161 residents were still in touch with the social worker with whom they had first made contact and who had arranged their accommodation. Table 5 shows the number of interviews these girls had before going into the Mother and Baby Home. It will be seen that in 45 per cent of these cases the social workers had had little or no opportunity to make a sound judgement of their clients' personality and circumstances, although three-quarters of these clients had contacted them before the end of the sixth month. If residents had seen more than one social worker there was even less chance that they would be well known to whichever one had arranged their accommo-

Table 5

Number of interviews with social workers before entering Home

Interviews	No. of girls	%
None	5	3.1
1 or 2	67	41.7
3 or 4	54	33.5
5 or more	30	18.6
no information	5	3.1
TOTAL	161	100

dation. Only 39 per cent of these residents had seen the first worker three or more times, while 33 per cent had had a similar number of interviews with the second worker.

THE FRAMEWORK OF THE SERVICE OFFERED BY THE HOMES

The Period for Which Accommodation was Available
Two Homes offered accommodation as and when it was necessary. One was a Home for schoolgirls, where the length of stay both before and after the baby's birth was arranged to suit each girl's educational needs. The other was a local health authority Home admitting residents at any stage of pregnancy and allowing them to stay as long as they liked. Both before and after the baby's birth residents could live in this Home and go out to work and sometimes mothers who kept their child were given employment in the Home.

In all the other Homes accommodation was usually provided for approximately three months; residents were admitted during the last six weeks of their pregnancy and expected to stay until the baby was about six weeks old. Five Homes made no definite ruling on the length of stay though the matrons reported that social workers almost invariably booked their clients for periods of six weeks before and after the baby's birth. The other sixteen Homes laid down a minimum period of stay both before and after the birth. Ante-natally the period ranged from three to twelve weeks. Post-natally the stay was fixed at a minimum of six weeks, and residents were required to extend their stay if suitable arrangements had not already been made for the baby. Two Homes permitted mothers who were keeping their baby to leave whenever they wished, and in three others they could leave between two days and two weeks early. These were the formal rules and the Homes varied greatly in their willingness to depart from them. At one extreme, exceptions to the normal ruling were rare and conceded grudgingly only in the most unusual circumstances. At the other, the degree of flexibility was so great that the only determinant of a resident's length of stay was her period of need for accommodation.

Admission Criteria

All the Homes had some conditions of eligibility governing the admission of residents. These can be grouped in the following way:

1. *Marital Status*: Sixteen Homes were for single women and girls only. In six of them a married woman might be accepted in exceptional circumstances, though many matrons expressed the view that illegitimate pregnancy was less excusable in a woman who was or had been married, than in a single girl. The married women were regarded as a bad influence on the others ('because of their dirty talk', explained one matron) and matrons were unwilling to have them in the Homes.

2. *Number of Previous Pregnancies*: Seven Homes, including the four provided by local health authorities, would admit residents with any number of previous pregnancies. Otherwise first pregnancies only was the general rule. Each subsequent pregnancy reduced the number of Homes to which an applicant would be admitted though the normal ruling might be waived if an applicant had not been to a Mother and Baby Home before. Few Matrons would readmit anyone who had previously been in their own Home, believing that if a resident had failed to learn anything from her first visit she was unlikely to benefit from a second.

3. *Religion*: Half the Homes made a stipulation about an applicant's faith. Basically this turned on the issue of whether or not the applicant was a Roman Catholic. The two Roman Catholic Homes would accept members of the Catholic faith only, though one accepted non-Catholic applicants if the putative father was a Roman Catholic and Catholic adopters were wanted for the baby. Three Homes said bluntly 'no RCs', but the more common attitude was summed up by the matron who said 'We find RCs a bit spikey because we can't help them very much, so we don't encourage them unless they've lapsed.' Another matron expressed herself 'wary of cults' but was prepared to admit girls if they 'understand they are not to circulate their literature while they are here.'

4. *Age*: Two Homes catered specifically for young girls under 17, and two specifically excluded them. A few matrons expressed a prefer-

ence for a particular age range, but this criterion of admission was probably set aside more frequently than any other. Sympathy was more readily extended to young girls, though one matron preferred to take the older applicants because 'Well, how shall I put it, it's less animal somehow. There's usually some sort of relationship with the man, and the girl imagines she's been in love with him.'

5. *Physically or Mentally Handicapped Girls*: Exact information about handicapped applicants was difficult to obtain because Homes were rarely asked to take them. Some matrons were definitely against admitting them, and gave lack of trained staff as the reason. A rather larger number were prepared to accept handicapped applicants provided they could manage the normal life of the Home. Few Homes would take epileptic cases, and several matrons suggested that a special Home was needed for such cases.

6. *Venereal Disease*: Generally Homes required applicants to be tested for venereal disease before admission. There were several complaints that general practitioners were unco-operative in this respect, and two instances were given of venereal disease being discovered in a resident who had presented a clear certificate. Subsequent enquiry into these cases showed that the tests had never been done.

7. *Girls on Probation and from Approved School*: Four Homes had a definite bar against all such cases, but in others a separate decision would be made on each case history. One matron liked to have these 'naughty ones'.

8. *Nationality*: One Home only took a non-British girl if her social worker would accept responsibility for arranging the baby's future, and in another, each case was discussed by the committee. Otherwise all Homes admitted applicants of any nationality.

9. *Place of Residence*: One local health authority Home was open to local residents only, and two gave priority to local cases. One voluntary Home refused all local cases.

10. *Background*: Whilst this was not amongst the formal criteria of eligibility laid down in any Home in the survey area, it was clear that it influenced admission. Two or three matrons described themselves as 'choosey' about applicants' backgrounds. Several others commented that although they themselves were willing to accept anyone, they tended to have a particular type of resident sent to them. It emerged from the interviews with the social workers that certain matrons were

generally regarded as particularly successful in forming good relationships with certain types of girls, and, as we have seen, it was common practice amongst social workers to try to select a Home for a client with this in mind.

The number and type of admission criteria employed by different Homes varied considerably. So too did the strictness with which they were applied; in some instances it seemed that certain rules had almost ceased to operate in practice. The local authority Homes, as might be expected, from their general duty to care for mothers and young children, were amongst those with the freest admission policy. So, too, was the Salvation Army Home, following the general Army policy of accommodating any unmarried mother in need, whatever her circumstances. Amongst the matrons of the other voluntary Homes, however, the general uncertainty about Mother and Baby Homes and the lack of agreement on their purpose became evident. There was a conflict of views between those who believed that the door of the Church should stand open to anyone, and those who held that there was much to be gained from some degree of selection.

Admission criteria seemed to serve two functions. On the one hand, they achieved the positive objective of defining the particular group for which the service was provided: schoolgirls, local residents, or Roman Catholics. On the other hand, they operated negatively to exclude those with certain characteristics: a previous pregnancy, a history of delinquency, or again local residents or Roman Catholics. The positive functioning of admission criteria was evident in only a few Homes. Far more commonly conditions of eligibility operated in the negative or exclusive sense, and this raises the issue of how well a service can be defined in terms of those it is *not* for. It is not possible to define Mother and Baby Homes simply as catering for unmarried mothers. Nor (with a few exceptions) can they be described as catering for particular groups of unmarried mothers. All that can be said, is that Mother and Baby Homes are for unmarried mothers unless they possess certain apparently undesirable characteristics. It would seem that the original motive for an exclusive admission policy was an attempt to distinguish the deserving from the undeserving with the aim of limiting the scope of the service to the former group. This is a philosophy which in other social services is long out-dated and its continued existence in Mother and Baby Homes may well stem from the punitive element still evident amidst conflicting social attitudes towards unmarried mothers.

Perhaps what emerges most clearly, however, is the need for Homes to define their purpose. Their present uncertainty of purpose is clearly seen in the different attitudes towards admission policies and length of stay. Mother and Baby Homes must decide the scope of their services in these terms, but exactly how they do so inevitably determines the sort of service they can provide. The very fact that formal policies on these matters were sometimes almost meaningless in practice is argument enough that they need to be reviewed.

5

THE RESIDENTS IN THE HOMES

The data from the residents' questionnaires showed that the Homes catered for unmarried mothers of widely differing circumstances. There were single girls expecting their first baby, and married women with two or three legitimate children. There were girls who could barely read or write, college students and a teacher. Their ages ranged from thirteen to thirty-nine, and their jobs from factory and domestic workers to fully qualified nursing sisters. Answering such a wide range of needs presents real problems to Mother and Baby Homes. But although it is quite possible that one resident of a Home might have nothing, apart from her extra-marital pregnancy, in common with any of the others, certain characteristics are likely to be shared by the majority of residents.

Marital Status
The first of these is marital status. Mother and Baby Homes cater almost exclusively for single girls. Only six out of the 240 residents had been married. Two were widows; the other four were either separated or divorced from their husbands.

Number of Pregnancies
Ninety-two per cent of the residents were having their first pregnancy. Only eighteen had already had another child, and four of these were married women with children of their marriage. Fourteen single girls said they had had another baby, including one who had had two previous illegitimate children. This figure of previous illegitimate pregnancies is almost certainly too low. The matrons told us of two other residents who had already had a child, but even they did not always have full histories for all their residents, and one resident who admitted to a previous pregnancy was in a Home which firmly excluded such cases.

Nationality

Ninety per cent of the residents were from the United Kingdom. Amongst the others were 3 girls with one British parent, 9 who described themselves as Irish, and 6 West Indians. The others were 2 German girls who had become pregnant in England, and a Maltese girl who came here on discovering her pregnancy.

Age

It is the young unmarried mother who goes into a Mother and Baby Home. A comparison of our data with that on all illegitimate maternities showed highly significant differences in the age of the mothers.[1] The Registrar General's Population Tables show that 60 per cent of all illegitimate maternities occur in women under the age of 25, and 21 per cent in women of 30 and over. Yet half the residents we saw were under 20. A further 29 per cent were under 25 and less than 4 per cent aged 30 or over. Our total sample was, however, weighted towards the lower end of the scale because of the two Homes for girls under 17. Both of these were in the southern region so it is probable that the age range of residents admitted to all Mother and Baby Homes is nearer to that of the northern sample on its own. Even here a high proportion of the residents were young girls, although none of the northern Homes catered exclusively for them.

Table 6

Residents of Northern Region Homes by age

Age	No. of Residents	%
Under 20	67	46.2
20–24	53	36.5
25–29	14	9.7
30 and over	3	2.1
No information	8	5.5
TOTAL	145	100

It is widely believed that social workers tend to encourage the young girls in their case loads to go into a Mother and Baby Home and that they do in fact arrange residential care for a disproportionately large number of these cases. This was not borne out by our evidence. We compared the ages of mothers in our sample with those found in

[1] Registrar General 1964.

each of two studies of unmarried mothers consulting social workers about an illegitimate pregnancy.[1] In neither case was there any significant difference, even though we used the figures for our total sample in the comparison. The ages of the girls we interviewed have been grouped here according to the Registrar General's classification to facilitate comparisons with other studies, but his gives a slightly misleading interpretation of our data. The detailed tables lodged at the N.C.U.M.C.[2] and the N.I.S.W.T.[3] show that the peak ages were 17–21 years. This five year age-group accounted for 60 per cent of all the residents, and 64 per cent of the northern sample. The average age of the total sample was 20.1 years. The most common single age was 19, and the median was 18.6 years.

Occupations
Table 7 shows the jobs held by the girls when they became pregnant. These it is reasonable to assume would represent their normal occupation.

There were only two notable differences in occupations between the regions. One was the predictably higher percentage of schoolgirls and students in the south; 20 per cent against 6 per cent; the two Homes in the South for girls in full-time education accommodated girls from all over the country. The other was the proportionately larger number of factory workers in the north; 36 per cent compared with 16 per cent. The explanation for this lies in the different nature of the two regions. The southern area was largely rural, and urban centres were mainly market towns or centres of commerce. The northern region contained several large manufacturing and industrial towns.

Of the 196 girls who stated they were in some form of gainful employment when they became pregnant, only 50 (25.2 per cent) had a change of employment during their pregnancy and only 24 girls (12.2 per cent) actually changed to a different type of occupation.

The number of domestics rose from two to ten but little can be said about the figures we collected on change of occupation during pregnancy in the absence of any comparative data on job changes occurring during a nine month period amongst a similar group of non-pregnant single women. The main point of interest emerges for adoption societies concerned with matching the social class of adoptive

---
[1] Yelloly 1964, Ball 1962.
[2] National Council for the Unmarried Mother and her Child.
[3] National Institute for Social Work Training.

Table 7
Occupations of Residents

Occupation	No. of Residents	%
Factory	67	27.9
Office or clerical	41	17.1
Shop	22	9.2
Nurse (or student nurse)	17	7.1
Domestic	14	5.8
Hairdresser	9	3.8
Waitress	7	2.9
Other gainful employment	19	7.9
Schoolgirl	22	9.2
Student	6	2.5
Housewife	1	0.4
Unemployed	8	3.3
No information	7	2.9
TOTAL	240	100

parents and the natural mother on the basis of the latter's occupation. With only a quarter of the total employed sample changing employment and less than half of these taking jobs of a different type there is only weak evidence to support the assumption that unmarried mothers may be temporarily employed in jobs which give them a lower social status than normal.[1]

Relationship With the Putative Father

Although 76 per cent of the residents said that the putative father knew about the baby, they had little contact with him during their stay in the Mother and Baby Home. Because of the different rulings made by matrons on this point, the data is difficult to interpret, but only 26 per cent of the girls said that they had seen or heard from the baby's father since their admission.

During the group interviews we gained an impression that it was most often the young girls who had a stable relationship with the baby's father, and Table 8 shows that the young girls were more likely than the older ones to maintain contact with the baby's father while they were in the Home. More detailed study of the data revealed two peaks of contact; one amongst girls aged 16–17 years and the other in residents around 24–25 years old. The small numbers in the second group make the relevance of this finding doubtful.

[1] Goodacre 1966.

Table 8

Contact with Putative Father by Age of Resident

Residents Age Group	Total No. in age group	No. in touch with putative father	% of age group in touch with putative father
Under 20	124	43	34.7
20–24	70	9	12.9
25 and over	32	6	18.8
No information	14	2	14.3
TOTAL	240	60	25.0

History of Illegitimacy

During the pilot study we were repeatedly told how often the unmarried mothers themselves were illegitimate, and so we made this a specific point of enquiry in the main study. Matrons were not always fully informed about the circumstances of the residents' birth, but at least thirty girls were known to have been born illegitimate. This figure (12.5 per cent of all the residents) was more than twice as high as would have been expected in a normal population of girls of a similar age (5.94 per cent). Similarly, Thompson in a comparative study of married and unmarried women giving birth to their first child found that 10 per cent of the unmarried mothers were themselves illegitimate compared with only 3 per cent of the married women.[1] Why this should be so is a matter of conjecture. If as Gough[2] suggests the problems of a confused and unhappy childhood can be passed on through several generations, and that girls who were born illegitimate have a need 'to act out and try to understand their mother's behaviour towards themselves as infants', this has important bearings on the purpose of the Homes and is a compelling argument for providing a service which will include the provision of casework and psychiatric care.

Family Background

The majority of residents came from homes where both parents were alive and living together. Our figure of 68 per cent intact homes was somewhat higher than that of other recent studies[3] and we may have

[1] Thompson 1956.
[2] Gough 1964.
[3] Ball gives 62 per cent intact homes, Thompson 60 per cent and Yelloly 51 per cent.

slightly overestimated the number of intact families by assuming that parents living in the same town were actually living together. Sixty-nine residents were from homes that had been broken by the death or separation of their parents. Eight residents had lost both parents, a further 16 were motherless, and 31 had no fathers, and in 14 cases both parents were alive but living separately.

Whether the home was broken or intact the predominant family pattern was one of close contact between the unmarried mothers and their living parents. In nearly every case the parents knew about the baby, and very many of them had known since the early months of the pregnancy. Nine girls had concealed their pregnancy from both parents, and a further nineteen had told their mother but not their father. It was very rare for the secret to be kept from mother, though telling her had not always been easy. 'It broke my mother's heart when I told her,' said one girl. 'I never wanted to hurt my mother like I have done over this. I don't know how some girls can tell their mother twice. I could never tell mine again.'

Parents kept in touch with their daughters while they were in the Home. Almost two-thirds of the girls had seen their mother since admission. Mother was the one who visited and wrote letters most often, but even so half the girls had seen their father. Only thirteen had no contact with either parent during their stay, and some of these, at least, had only been in the Home a few days. Further evidence of family support is furnished by the number of girls who lived with their families throughout their pregnancy. Seventy four per cent were living with one or both parents when the baby was conceived, and 64 per cent were with them just before coming into the Home. Although 35 girls who were living with one or both parents when they became pregnant had moved away before entering the Home, 13 others who had conceived while living away from home went back to their parents.

Our information on family structure came from the residents' questionnaires and we had little direct opportunity to assess the quality of family relationships. When the girls spoke of their families during the interviews it was usually with a warmth that suggested stability and affection. This was particularly so when they talked of their mothers. An assessment of the Mother and Baby Home, even a favourable one, was often rounded off by regret of the necessity to leave the family home, and a wistful comment that 'there's no one like your Mam, is there?' There was no doubt how much the girls valued their parents' support. 'I don't know what I would have done if my parents hadn't been behind me' was a common attitude, and there was shocked sympathy for girls whose parents had rejected them. The others thought it 'dreadful when your parents won't stand behind you. I mean to say, they can't be proper loving parents if they let you down at a time like this, can they?'

The matrons, on the other hand, repeatedly threw doubt on the seeming normality of family relationships. They told us that time and again, even in the families which were apparently most stable and united, some evidence of strain or difficulty would emerge. Often there was said to be an underlying tension between the unmarried mother and one of her parents, or it was thought that the relationship between the parents themselves was unsatisfactory. Several matrons remarked on the number of girls who became pregnant shortly after their mother married for a second time.

It is difficult to know which of these pictures is the true one. Other studies have found evidence of poor relationships in intact families, but the results are not easy to interpret. Ball noted that out of 31 structurally intact families in her sample only 24 'could be described as ostensibly normal'. Thompson reported as a minimum estimate that one sixth of the unmarried mothers from intact homes had suffered an unhappy upbringing. Yelloly, on the other hand, and Anderson et al[1] point out that the quality of family relationships may be good even when the structure is not a normal one. In both these studies when the quality of relationships alone was considered, 'good' homes far outnumbered the 'bad' ones, and in neither study was it thought that the families under consideration presented 'an unduly psycho-pathological picture'. Clearly there is room for research into the interrelationship between family structure and the quality of relationships, and we need also to know how these two factors separately or together may contribute towards illegitimate maternity.

Plans After Leaving the Mother and Baby Home

1. *Living Arrangements*

Just over three quarters of the girls were returning to live with parents or relatives when they left the Home. This was what they wanted to do. They felt desperately sorry for the girls who could not go home. At a time like this 'you just want your Mother's love. That's the best thing. If you get back home, there's no one like your Mam and she's the best person to be with'.

[1] Anderson, et al. 1960.

The living arrangements planned by the girls for when they left the Home are shown in Table 9. Fifty-five residents had no definite intention of going to live with parents or relatives, and it was generally agreed that having no home to return to was a severe problem. No one, however, left the Mother and Baby Home without having somewhere to go, and matrons and social workers were said to be very kind and helpful to girls who faced this difficulty.

Table 9

Plans for Living Arrangements on Leaving

	No. of residents	%
Parents or relatives	185	77.1
Friends	8	3.3
Alone	7	2.9
Residential job	4	1.7
Temporary arrangement until marrying or finding a residential job	4	1.7
Residential Home or Hostel	3	1.3
Boyfriend	2	0.8
Don't know	20	8.3
No information	7	2.9
TOTAL	240	100

2. *The Girls Who Were Planning to Keep their Babies*

Of the 40 residents who were planning to keep their babies, 19 were returning to live with their parents when they left the Mother and Baby Home. Seven did not know where they would live, and the others were making a variety of arrangements which included living with friends, living on their own, and going into a residential hostel.

In the great majority of cases the mother was intending to have the baby living with her. Only four were planning to place the child with foster parents and four others did not know where the baby would live. Only six mothers, however, thought that they themselves would be looking after the baby during the day. Most girls were intending to go out to work, and they had to make other arrangements for the care of the baby. Usually they hoped the baby would be looked after by relatives or placed in a day nursery.

3. Jobs

A third of the residents were sure of a job waiting for them when they left the Mother and Baby Home, and in all but six cases they were returning to work for a previous employer. Finding work was a worry to other residents, not necessarily because of a possible shortage of vacancies but because of the difficulty of explaining an unstamped insurance card to a potential employer. They thought there was bound to be prejudice against them if they confessed to an illegitimate pregnancy and they were frightened they would be forced into low grade, badly paid jobs that no one else would take.

Differences Between the Regions

There were few differences between the residents of the northern and southern Homes, but there did seem to be a regional difference in the prevalent attitude towards illegitimacy. All the factors which might reflect the force of social pressures were more marked in the south than in the north. There were proportionately more residents in the southern region than in the north who concealed their pregnancy from their family. The residents from the south were more likely to have moved away from home during pregnancy and less likely to return to their parents on leaving the Mother and Baby Home. During their stay in the Home they were less likely than those in the north to have contact with friends and relatives. They were more likely to have changed jobs during their pregnancy and less likely to have one to return to when they left the Home.

The differences between regions were small in themselves, but added together they suggested that the unmarried mothers in the southern Homes had suffered more than those in the north from the social stigma attached to illegitimacy. This strengthened a similar impression received from the group interviews. The need to get away from the neighbours was a problem which exercised the residents in the southern Homes far more frequently than those in the north, and the great majority of those who hoped and believed they had concealed their condition were in the south. We never heard in the south, as we did in the north, of work mates who had a collection before a girl left, or of neighbours who knitted for the baby, or sent magazines and chocolates when a girl was in the Home.

This in no sense implied that an extra-marital pregnancy was condoned in the north. Far from it. The unmarried mothers were left in no doubt of their neighbours' disapproval, and they themselves felt they warranted it. But with the disapproval of their conduct went sympathy with its consequences, and the sum of these attitudes was a willingness to ease the difficulties of an unhappy situation with offers of practical kindness. An illegitimate pregnancy might be equally wrong in the north or the south, but to the girls in the northern Homes it was less of a disgrace.

6

THE MATERIAL STANDARDS

GENERAL FEATURES

Mother and Baby Homes do not advertise themselves as such to passers-by. Two Homes did hint at some institutional function by displaying notices; one warning 'Keep off the grass', the other 'No high heels'. Otherwise there was nothing to distinguish them from the other houses in the neighbourhood. Usually the Homes were in a built-up area in or near the centre of the town, and all of them had easy access to local shops and bus services. None of the Homes were purpose built and they were usually in large old residential houses adapted to the purpose with varying degrees of success. All the Homes had at least a small garden or yard, and four had sizeable grounds. Many of the gardens were walled or well-screened with trees and bushes, giving a sense of quietness and privacy even in the middle of a town.

Amongst the twenty-three Homes visited three stand out vividly, as clean, light, well-decorated and comfortably furnished. Their attractive and welcoming appearance contrasted sharply with the gloom and shabbiness which made the others so depressing. Very often the nature of the buildings frustrated attempts to make them homely. Large, draughty, old-fashioned houses with high ceilings and rambling corridors cannot easily be scaled down to give the sense of warmth and intimacy associated with 'home'. The layout of some of the houses, particularly those in which two or more buildings had been knocked into one, was confusing and made them difficult to run. In one Home two parts of the building were linked by a bathroom with a door at either end. In another the residents had to go through the nursery to reach their sitting-room. An unsuitable and even dangerous feature of many houses was the steep, narrow staircases leading to top floor bedrooms, or basements housing a Chapel or laundry. Even when covered in non-slip lino, such stairs were difficult for expectant mothers to climb, and in two Homes the hand-rails were broken. Old houses like these are expensive to heat, and several that we visited in the winter were very cold. They are also costly to maintain. So much money was needed for structural repairs that there was little left for furniture or decorating, and matrons shared a longing to furnish their Homes with something better and more comfortable than other people's throw-outs.

In some Homes everything had been done within the limits of the buildings and the available money to make the house attractive. Members of the staff had spent their own time and energy painting and decorating, and they had begged friends for carpets and curtains. If similar effort and imagination had been expended on all Homes many more could have been attractive. One of these had been largely re-built as a Mother and Baby Home just after the war. It was potentially a pleasant house, but the heavy cream and chocolate brown paint and the dim lights, shared one between two cubicles in the bedrooms, made it seem to one resident 'just like a prison when you first come in'.

In the next section of the chapter individual features of the Homes are considered in detail. Since there are no officially recognized standards for Mother and Baby Homes, the adequacy of facilities in the Homes we visited has been measured against a leaflet on material standards published by the National Council for the Unmarried Mother and Her Child.

STANDARDS OF ACCOMMODATION

Halls
Halls were one of the worst features of the Homes, dismal and bleak and often smelling strongly of cooking, washing or floor-polish. Inevitably the newcomer's first reaction was a bad one, and improvements in the hall could probably do more than anything else to relieve the impression of general dreariness.

Living Rooms
Most Homes had separate dining- and sitting-rooms, but in six one large room served as both. A third room when available for the residents was used for quiet activities, for entertaining visitors, or, in one case, as a smoking room. Living-room furniture was worn and clumsy.

Sometimes it was even broken, and in one Home the interviewer was warned not to sit on a settee that was unsafe. Footrests were sometimes provided for the expectant mothers, but chairs were often uncomfortable and unsuitable for them. Even with their drab furnishings most living rooms were relaxing, but in three Homes two rows of chairs marched stiffly down the middle of the room. In four Homes the rooms were too small for the numbers they might have to accommodate, and when the Homes were full, expectant and newly delivered mothers sat on the floor.

Kitchen Premises
Kitchen premises varied greatly from the large and rambling to the small and compact. There was a similar variation in the standard of equipment; in nine Homes we noted modern cookers, easily cleaned working tops and labour-saving gadgets, but almost as many had to make do with old-fashioned stoves and sinks and scrubbed tables.

Laundry Premises
One Home was completely equipped with commercial machinery and three others had excellent facilities; the walls and floors were tiled, there were modern and efficient washing and drying machines, and good airing and ironing facilities. One of these laundries had been recently modernized with a grant from a charitable trust. The old one, said the Matron, had been 'mediaeval'. This was almost true of some of the existing laundries we visited. Nine were noted as old-fashioned or poorly equipped. Some of these had no washing machines or driers and amongst the out-dated equipment in use were old-fashioned boilers and wringers, flat irons, and in one Home—wooden sinks.

Nurseries
Typically, the nursery was large, light and airy, and cots were trimmed and furniture painted. Even here, however, standards were not universally high; the worst nursery was a little room without any outside windows. Only one of the twelve Homes in which babies slept in the nursery at night provided both day and night nurseries. In as many as seven Homes we suspected that the nursery would be overcrowded if the Home was full. When we visited one Home which had more than its quota of residents, some mothers were feeding their babies in the sluice room. In none of the nurseries was it possible to have privacy when feeding the baby.

Bedrooms
There was at least one single room in each of twelve Homes, but bedrooms were usually shared; three to five residents in a room was a common arrangement. Generally residents liked sharing rooms. It was 'fun'—'You can have a giggle and a talk and forget your problems for a while', and it was a comfort to be with others 'when you want a good cry'. The shared rooms offered little privacy to those who did want it. Only in one Home were there curtains to draw round each bed. In another residents slept in separate cubicles, and this combination of privacy and companionship was appreciated.

As elsewhere in the Homes, the standard of furniture in the bedrooms was generally low. Old iron bedsteads were so common that to see wooden headboards was a surprise. Two Homes provided attractive wardrobe and dressing table units for each resident, but nine Homes were acutely short of cupboard and drawer space. One matron warned residents to bring as few clothes as possible because there was nowhere to keep them. Wardrobes, cupboards and drawers had to be shared, and only one Home provided individual lockers and keys in which residents could keep any personal valuables.

Sanitary Provision
By the standards recommended by the National Council for the Unmarried Mother and Her Child, sanitary provision was inadequate. Five Homes had less than the suggested number of baths for the size of the Home, and eleven were short of lavatories. In seven Homes some bedrooms had wash-hand basins, but only three Homes provided them in all bedrooms.

The general picture was worse than these figures suggest. The use of existing facilities was frequently limited because a bath, a washbasin and a lavatory were in the same room. In some instances, too, these facilities were inconveniently situated. In one Home there were no washing facilities in the wing housing the residents' bedrooms, and hot water had to be fetched in jugs from downstairs. Usually the lavatory reserved for staff use was upstairs and at night in Homes where provision was inadequate, residents had to go downstairs to a second lavatory. In another Home a lavatory cubicle for use during the night had been constructed in a dormitory.

There was little privacy for washing. Sometimes there would be two or three unscreened wash-basins in a row and only in one Home were the wash-basins in the bedroom screened. In another Home with two baths and several wash-basins in one room, wooden partitions screened the sides of the baths, but the front of the cubicles were covered only by a piece of torn sacking.

Household Equipment

We did not ask specific questions about household equipment, but sometimes either the staff or the residents mentioned particular requirements. Several Homes wanted electric mixers and vacuum cleaners, whilst a few were short of such mundane equipment as cloths and brushes. Several needed new cooking utensils and tableware, and when we had lunch in one Home, there were not enough glasses to go round. Two matrons told us that they had spent their own money buying attractive sets of crockery for the Home.

Staff Accommodation

Staff accommodation was generally poor. For residential staff the Mother and Baby Home is their personal home for the major part of the year; as well as somewhere to sleep, they need privacy to relax during off-duty time, and the opportunity to entertain their friends. In common with the Williams Committee, we found that even when there was adequate provision for the matron the needs of assistant staff were largely ignored. Four Homes provided the matron with a self-contained flatlet and one with her own house. In one Home the staff lived in a separate house, but otherwise matrons and assistants had nothing more than bed-sitting rooms and possibly a communal lounge. Many bed-sitting rooms were too small for their dual role, and the staff sitting-room frequently had to serve as an office and in one Home as the residents' dining and television room. Only two Homes provided guest rooms for the staff, and there were no separate cooking facilities apart from those in the matrons' flats.

REVIEW OF MATERIAL STANDARDS

The staff deplored the poor material standards of their Homes and saw them as an additional obstacle to an already difficult job. Old, rambling houses in poor repair were exhausting and unrewarding to manage and difficult to keep clean. They were also depressing to work in; this had its effect on the morale of staff and residents alike. The residents frequently mentioned the depressing condition of the Homes. So often their first impression of the Home confirmed their worst fears that they were coming to 'a workhouse' or 'a prison' and a common reaction was 'Oh God, have I got to stay here?' This was used as an argument against having a preliminary interview, some residents feeling that on an initial visit to the Homes they would have been so impressed by the gaunt and dreary shabbiness of the building that they would never have returned to discover the relief and support that came through living there. Two matrons believed that the bad conditions in the Homes were a hazard in their relationship with the residents; that girls who were sent to a depressing Home and set to work with old-fashioned equipment saw this as a deliberate attempt to punish them, and it created a barrier which staff had to overcome.

Even if the staff themselves had no wish to punish, there may be an element of truth in the residents' views. The bad conditions in Mother and Baby Homes may well be a reflection of a punitive attitude in the society which permits them to exist. Such an attitude is associated perhaps with the 'deterrent' approach to the care of unmarried mothers, identified in the first chapter, and the view that services for them should not be too generous. According to two matrons this view was typified in their management committees. Both committees steadfastly refused to sanction improvements the staff considered necessary, maintaining that anything was good enough for unmarried mothers.

While admitting the need for improvements, matrons sometimes reminded us that it would be wrong to judge a Home on the basis of the material standards alone. We agree with them that the quality of the staff is of far greater importance than the quality of the accommodation, and that good staff can overcome the most serious handicaps. Nevertheless, it is important that the truth of these arguments should not be used as an excuse for continued tolerance of inadequate provision, nor must they be allowed to detract from the force of the matrons' other arguments described above.

In general there was little to choose between the standards of accommodation provided by the different organizations responsible for the Homes. The best Home was run by a local health authority, but so was one of the worst. In an unpublished study of Mother and Baby Homes carried out in 1958, the Ministry of Health noted that standards in local health authority Homes were generally higher than in the voluntary Homes, and suggested that the reason for this might lie in the financial difficulties of voluntary organizations. Our evidence supports this view. Lack of finance was stated everywhere to be the overwhelming obstacle to improvement.

With the exception of the two committees already mentioned, matrons reported that management committees desired improvements as anxiously as they did, and they provided them when money permitted. Some Homes had already begun to raise their standards by small alterations carried out each year, but during the period covered by the survey there seems to have been a quickening in the pace of improvements. Ten Homes were planning improvements when we visited. It was perhaps a hopeful sign that nearly all the worst conditions described in this chapter were to be remedied, and the most extensive alterations were taking place where they were most badly needed; one Home was closing completely, one was to be entirely renovated and re-equipped, and a third was moving to new premises. Builders and decorators were at work in two of the Homes when we visited, and in several others large scale alterations were scheduled for the immediate future.

It may be that the movement towards better standards was stimulated by the National Council for the Unmarried Mother and Her Child's leaflet, and that this both emphasized the need for improvement and offered the necessary guide-lines towards it. The present survey revealed a real need for guidance in the planning of new Homes and the alteration of old ones. Few matrons or committee members were experienced in such matters, and some had never seen another Mother and Baby Home. Local health authorities might be consulted when improvements were in view, but their advice was not always found helpful, and it was suggested that local authorities had no greater experience of planning Mother and Baby Homes than the voluntary bodies. A need for an advisory service was evident and this should be provided by a central body with the opportunity to build up knowledge and experience of a wide variety of Homes. The National Council for the Unmarried Mother and her Child has already made a beginning but its service could develop further with advantage. Local Homes could play a part in this if they were more ready both to consult the National Council for the Unmarried Mother and Her Child and to report back to it when projects were completed. Although experience is in short supply, mutual co-operation would enable existing knowledge to be used to the maximum advantage.

7

THE PATTERN OF DAILY LIFE

This chapter and the two following deal with different aspects of the day-to-day life in the Homes. In various ways all three illustrate the lack of an agreed purpose in Mother and Baby Homes. Perhaps this is most clearly seen in the ill-defined status of the residents, which is discussed at the end of Chapter Nine.

The residents' anticipation of what life would be like in a Mother and Baby Home demonstrates how little known they are to the general public. Many unmarried mothers had never heard of such places. They, and their families, were aghast at the idea of their living in one. One girl's grandmother had cried when she heard her granddaughter was going to a Mother and Baby Home. 'They're just like the workhouse,' she told her, 'You'll be in the wash-house there.' The image of the Homes was generally an old-fashioned one of somewhere totally enclosed, where life was strictly regulated and work was hard and long. It was 'thought there'd be bars on the windows' and that the walls would be covered in notices. One resident had lit a cigarette in the car as she was driven to the Home thinking it would be her last until 'it was all over'. Many had believed that they would never be allowed to go out. The Homes of the residents' imagination were grim indeed and it is not surprising that the real ones were always better than expected, and often very much better.

DAILY ROUTINE

The pattern of the day, set by the babies' feeding times, was broadly similar in all the Homes. The greater part of the mornings until lunch time were spent on housework. After lunch there was usually a quiet period, and residents could rest if they wished. Nine matrons insisted that everyone should spend an hour or so lying on their beds. Following this there might be a handicraft or relaxation class but otherwise afternoons were free, and this was the most usual time for residents to be allowed to go out. Evenings were also free and residents could amuse themselves in the Home. For the mothers the day was a long one, beginning with the first feed around 5.30 or 6.00 a.m. and ending only when the babies were finally settled for the night between 10.30 and 11.00 p.m. Expectant mothers had a shorter day, rising about 7.00 or 7.30 and going to bed as early as they wished.

The same routine operated throughout the week. This caused some mild complaining amongst the residents. The weeks seemed to drag when every day was the same, and there was a general feeling that Sunday ought to be 'different' and a day to look forward to. In fact, Sunday was commonly 'the most boring day of the week'. Ten Homes would not allow visitors on Sundays, and in some the residents were not allowed out at all except to go to church. Two Homes placed severe restrictions on normal leisure time activities. Cards, games, the record player and the television were prohibited, and in one Home all Sunday newspapers were forbidden and the radio permitted for only an hour in the afternoon. In this Home the residents indignantly attacked what they termed staff hypocrisy. Residents were not allowed to cook meat, they complained, but they had to cook the potatoes: they could not do their own washing and ironing, but they had to wash and iron for the staff. If it was wrong in principle to work on Sundays, the residents concluded, then they should not have to do anything at all. In the other Home the residents were more tolerant of their restricted freedom. 'After all,' one of them explained, 'that's their [the staff's] Holy Day, you see.'

FOOD AND MEALS

The standard of food in the Homes was high. In twelve Homes the residents expressed unqualified approval of the food, and the meals we had in these Homes confirmed their good opinion. In the small minority of Homes where criticism was voiced, it was mainly the expectant mothers who complained that they did not get enough to eat, or that fatty or stodgy food gave them indigestion. In general, however, the food was said to be well cooked, plentiful and varied.

Residents usually helped to prepare meals and in about half the Homes they cooked the breakfast or the evening meal for themselves. Six Homes provided a cooked breakfast every day. In others there was usually just cereal and toast or bread and marmalade. Two Homes catered for individual preferences by allowing those who liked a full breakfast to cook bacon and eggs for themselves, and this sensible arrangement could be more widely practised. Half-way through the morning there was a break for a drink, and the main meal of the day was at midday. In the afternoons there was either a light tea about 4 o'clock, followed by a cooked supper, or a high tea around 5.30 p.m. and a light supper later in the evening. As at breakfast, two Homes allowed girls to choose and cook their own evening meal from food provided by the Home.

In three Homes residents could make themselves a cup of tea whenever they wished. This was very much appreciated, and it would be a simple matter to provide an electric kettle for the use of the residents in every Home. There were widespread complaints that residents did not receive their full daily allowance of cheap milk. The validity of the complaints was doubtful in view of the erroneous but prevalent impression that expectant and nursing mothers were entitled to one or even one and a half 'free' pints of milk each day. The supposed shortage of milk was, however, one of the main focuses of discontent, and it is interesting to note that in a Home for discharged Borstal boys, Miller found that milk consumption was astonishingly high, and that the quantity of milk consumed rose dramatically during periods of tension in the house.[1] All cause for complaint, however, would be removed if the practice of one Home visited during the pilot study was followed: all the residents were encouraged to help themselves to milk from the refrigerator as freely as they wished.

Storage space for residents' food was provided only in one Home, and it seemed that matrons did not always appreciate the need for occasional snacks between meals. Even in the Homes where food was good and plentiful many residents felt the need for a little extra between times. Normally they provided this for themselves, but three matrons would not allow food to be brought into the Home. The residents disregarded this rule, and cold baked beans and packets of crisps were consumed surreptitiously. The reason for such a ruling is difficult to see. If diets are necessary they should be prescribed by the doctor, not the matron.

HOUSEWORK

In all the Homes the residents shared in the housework, though the amount and type of work varied greatly. At one extreme the residents did little more than help with the washing-up and keep their rooms tidy. At the other they did all the work, cooking, cleaning, scrubbing

[1] Miller 1964.

and polishing. They stoked the boilers and served the staff, waiting on them at meals, turning down their beds at night, and doing their washing and ironing. The work the residents were given to do depended very much on the views of the matron. On the one hand, some matrons thought that newly delivered mothers and women nearing the end of a pregnancy tired easily and should not be asked to do much. On the other, we were told that scrubbing and polishing were good for pregnant women, and residents would have difficult confinements unless they were kept physically active.

During the course of the visits it became obvious that housework served a variety of purposes of which keeping the house clean was only one. Its most common function was a means of keeping the residents occupied; either to take their minds off their worries, or to prevent them from getting bored. In one Home the heavy load of housework formed part of a definite policy to reform the residents' values and attitudes to life. It could also serve a teaching function for matrons who wanted residents to learn some of the skills of housekeeping. Three matrons told us that few of their residents had any knowledge of this when they arrived.

In half the Homes housework began before breakfast with a task such as laying a fire, or peeling vegetables. The main work followed during the rest of the morning. In a third of the Homes there was little to do and the residents said they finished within an hour, or an hour and a half. In another third, work was planned to last all morning, and an extra job was found for anyone finishing early. The housework was usually shared out by a member of staff on a daily or weekly rota. This ensured that each resident took her turn at the less pleasant jobs and that the work could be graded, the lighter jobs going to those nearest their confinement. Mothers did not always share in the housework, as some matrons considered them to be fully occupied in caring for their babies.

Not surprisingly the residents' attitude to housework was related to the amount and type of work they were expected to do. Occasionally a resident objected on principle to doing any work because she was paying for her stay, and one of these assured the rest of the group that married women in private Maternity Homes were waited on hand and foot for only £6 per week. In general, however, the residents did not seem to mind the work, and even welcomed it as a way of helping time to pass. They laughed when we asked them if they thought they had to work too hard. In reply to this question one girl described her job 'as just really hanging around in the laundry'. Others did find the work hard even when there was not much of it to do. 'It's not just tickling the top of it,' they told us, 'you have to be really thorough' and some confessed they felt 'really jiggered up' afterwards. But they had the rest of the day to recover, and if they did 'moan now and again, no one really meant it'.

In eight Homes housework was considered a real grievance. The residents complained that the work was hard, long and unsuitable. They were told that they must not lift things, yet they had to move and clean behind heavy pieces of furniture, and carry trays of crockery and glasses filled with water. They were told not to stretch but they had to dust the tops of the wardrobes and climb up ladders to wash the paint. One resident wrote on her questionnaire that they should not be 'made to work so hard. I'm not lazy but it really is a bit too much to expect girls in our condition to be on our hands and knees all morning', and another suggested they should be given 'suitable jobs to keep you active, but only active not to make you feel tired and backachey!'

Where the object of the work was clearly to fill in time rather than to keep the house clean, there was a feeling of frustration and futility at senseless cleaning; spinning out for two hours a job that could be done in one, because work could not stop until twelve o'clock, and 'spring-cleaning every day' in an unused nursery, or a chapel which was only used for ten minutes each day. An additional source of resentment lay in the inspection of work by a member of the staff. According to the residents this was carried out with unnecessary thoroughness; even the keyholes were said to be checked in one Home. Sometimes the reason for such strictness was discussed by the group, and one resident ventured a suggestion that hygiene was especially important in a house full of babies. 'Yes, but not in the boiler house,' came the tart reply from a girl who polished the boiler every day, 'you don't put babies in the boiler house.' It was depressing, the residents told us, because 'however hard you try the staff still nag you, and it makes you feel that you don't want to try again the next day'. One matron countered this by declaring that the residents did *not* try. 'If they did,' she said, 'I wouldn't have to natter at them.'

It was difficult to judge the validity of the residents' complaints. There was little chance to see them at work, and as the bulk of the work fell on expectant mothers the work load at any one time was partly dependent on the relative numbers of mothers and expectant mothers in the Home. Two other studies of Mother and Baby Homes concluded that 'in general, the tasks done by the girls are not arduous and where necessary they are adjusted according to physical ability'.[1] Although this seemed to be true of the majority of Homes we visited, we did think it likely that in five Homes at least the housework was excessive or unsuitable in character, particularly in view of the generally accepted policy requiring expectant mothers to come into the Home several weeks before the confinement in order to have a period of rest and relaxation.

The appropriateness of housework to the physical condition of the residents is not the only aspect of this subject which might be questioned, and in our view the Homes should reconsider the policy of using housework as a means of occupation to the extent that they do. The policy was justified to us on the grounds that residents were asked to do no more than a married woman would do in her own home. Although married women do work of a similar nature we felt the analogy was not a true one; the context of the married woman's work is so different. There is no compulsion on her to complete a certain job to a certain standard within a specified time. She is free to leave some work for another day, and she may have friends or relatives to help her. It is also arguable that even the housekeeping and cleaning done single-handed by a married woman for her family is less arduous than using inadequate equipment to clean part of a large, shabby building housing fifteen to twenty people.

It seemed likely that two other factors also helped to explain why housework was such a dominant feature of the daily life, though neither of these was mentioned. The first was economy. Only half the Homes had domestic help, which is expensive and often hard to obtain. The residents provide an accessible and cheap alternative source of labour. To use them as such we considered was unreasonable. The residents may fairly be asked to help with washing up, to make their beds and to keep their rooms tidy, but they should not be used to replace hired domestic help, and where necessary the fees of the Homes should be raised to pay for this. Secondly, it seemed that historical influences played a part in the prevalence of housework. In the days of the Rescue Homes it appears to have been taken for granted that domestic work was one of the few activities to which penitents were suited. Though this attitude itself has gone, traces of it linger. Three matrons did suggest housework was unsatisfactory. As an alternative they tried to offer their residents a chance to use their own particular skills while in the Home. A nurse might be asked to help with the babies or with medical examinations and a bank clerk to do some of

[1] Hall and Howes 1965, Ministry of Health 1958.

the accounts. A secretary might be asked to do some typing, and in one Home a girl who was studying domestic science cooked the lunch on Saturdays. The matrons found this worked well, they thought the residents liked to feel they were being useful, and appreciated the chance to keep in touch with their normal work.

OTHER ORGANIZED ACTIVITIES

A common problem to matrons in Mother and Baby Homes noted also by Hall and Howes is the provision of suitable activities for the residents. Matrons generally felt that the residents' life was dreary, dull and monotonous. Yet it was very difficult to find something which the residents would enjoy, and which would suit the wide variety of ages, interest and abilities found in most Mother and Baby Homes. The Home for schoolgirls had less of a problem than most as so much of the day was taken up with lessons. One of the other Homes had achieved a successful variety of activities including films, outings, parties, discussion groups, socials, plays and sing-songs. Some of the residents laughed a little at these group activities, at the same time admitting they enjoyed them, and that life was never dull. In the other Homes, apart from the housework, there was little for residents to do. In a few there were sewing or handicraft classes, and in the church Homes the Vicar or Chaplain held weekly discussion groups. Otherwise attempts to occupy or entertain the residents were limited to the occasional party or film-show.

Other types of residential Homes besides Mother and Baby Homes face a similar problem, and more needs to be known about how to offer residents something to do without either using them as cheap labour or compelling them to join in artificial jollifications which seem a little silly to everyone. Mother and Baby Homes have the added difficulty of catering for residents of widely differing ages. A generation of interests can separate the oldest and the youngest residents in a Home, and the routine and activities suitable for one group are quite inappropriate to the other. To offset this, Mother and Baby Homes do have one advantage over other types of residential Home in the planning of suitable activities. All the residents share in common the fact that they are having an illegitimate baby. Classes in preparation for the confinement, talks, and discussion groups on such topics as adoption, fostering, day nursery facilities and social security benefits would be relevant to everyone, and at least some residents would probably find them interesting and helpful. Few Homes even attempted group activities on these lines, and none exploited the possibilities in full. This seemed a real opportunity lost.

FREE TIME AND TIME TO GO OUT

Residents were free whenever they had finished their housework and there were no classes to attend. In the average Home this meant that residents could do as they wished nearly every afternoon and most evenings, though they might have to stay indoors. Freedom to go out of the Home, or even into the garden, in extreme cases was regulated. The common pattern was to allow residents to go out for two or three hours each afternoon. Several Homes were less generous than this, but in contrast, one Home allowed the residents to come and go as they wished from lunch time until nine or ten o'clock in the evening. Few of the other Homes were willing for residents to go out in the evenings unless they were with visitors or going to see a mother in hospital. A number of Homes had residents in the care of a Children's Department and their time to go out might be limited at the request of their child care officer.

There were also other rulings affecting the freedom of the residents to go out of the Home. Some of the matrons stipulated that residents should ask permission before going out. This might be a mere formality, but in one Home the residents said that they were not 'really expected to ask all that often' and permission was not always granted. Other matrons liked to be told where residents were going and when they returned, and some ruled that expectant mothers must go out in groups of twos or threes. This, the residents considered reasonable, because 'somebody might have a mis. (miscarriage), or go into labour or something'. There might also be restrictions on what residents could do once they were out of the Home. Amongst a range of forbidden activities noted in four Homes were bus rides, visits to certain shops or parts of the town, and meetings with friends or even parents. This last rule, which local girls found hard to bear, was made for the sake of the majority of residents who could only see their families at weekends. There would usually be trouble if residents were found going against these restrictions, but one matron maintained that when she was off duty she should be off duty, and if she happened to see residents breaking rules, she looked the other way.

The mothers' freedom to go out was limited by the natural tie of caring for their babies, but many of the expectant mothers fretted against the restrictions, complaining that they felt 'shut in' and 'cut off'. They found it difficult to understand why they had to stay in, particularly in the evenings, because 'nobody is going dancing, or off to pubs in our state, and we haven't any money, so why don't they let us go out?—We can only go for a walk or to the pictures'. While the majority expressed views like this, there were many other residents who were not so keen to go out. Some who lived locally preferred to stay in the Home; going shopping increased their chances of 'being seen'. Others could not find much enjoyment in going out because 'we feel so guilty that we feel everybody must be looking at us'. And there were a number who were quite content to stay in the Home: it was 'a real effort' to get ready to go out, and they were too tired to go 'lumbering round the town'.

The different views on the sufficiency of free time appeared to be related more closely to the overall degree of freedom allowed to the residents in the Home than to the actual number of hours during which they were permitted to go out. In the Homes where the day was rigidly time-tabled, and the residents had little opportunity to please themselves, there was a strong wish for more time outside the Home, even when the hours allowed were comparatively generous. Yet in the Homes where the atmosphere was free, residents stayed in even when they could have gone out. As several of them suggested, the real need was not necessarily to go out, but to feel free to do so. This point is very relevant for matrons and committees who set the limits of freedom in the Homes, and we felt that many could be much more generous in this respect than they are at present.

8

RULES

All communities need rules, to maintain order, to balance the interests of the individuals or groups who make up the community, and to ease the problems of administration. In addition to these general rules, communities or institutions such as Mother and Baby Homes, which have been established to fulfil a specific function, may employ special rules designed to further their particular purpose. Most of the rules in the Homes visited could be explained in these terms. This chapter deals first with the rules and the residents reactions to them. Then the maintenance of order and some of the influences on the rules are discussed.

CONCERNING VISITORS

Visitors
All the Homes allowed parents to visit their daughters. Only one Home made an exception to this, and the girl's father was supposed to obtain the matron's permission first. Visits from other relatives and friends, with the possible exception of children under fourteen or fifteen who were sometimes excluded as a safeguard against infection, were also generally permitted. In regard to boy friends, however, each Home made its own ruling. This was often so hedged about by conditions and qualifications that it is almost impossible to draw an overall picture.

Some matrons thought that residents could benefit from masculine company and admiration and in four Homes there was no ruling at all against visits from boy friends. Other matrons tried to distinguish 'genuine boy friends' from 'just ordinary camp followers'. An attempt at a similar distinction seemed to lie behind rules which allowed boy friends to visit only if they had the permission of the girl's parents or if they were accompanied by their own or the girl's parents. Other matrons, though they were prepared to allow the baby's father to visit, provided he was not a married man, would not let other boy friends come to the Home. They gave no reasons for this policy beyond the fact that visits from boy friends seemed 'inadvisable'. One matron did say that she thought there must be something odd about a boy who took out a girl who was having another man's baby. In a third of the Homes, visits from boy friends, whether or not they were the father of the child, were forbidden completely. In three Homes, an attitude towards male visitors in general seemed evident. There is the Home already mentioned where the residents' fathers had to ask permission to visit. In this Home and another one, brothers could not come without special permission, and in the third Home the residents complained that even the husbands of friends and relatives who came to see them were looked at 'with suspicion'. The matrons explained the ban on visits from male friends by saying that the residents needed a time away from men 'to sort themselves out'. Two simply said that they had enough to do without being bothered by 'a lot of young boys littering round the place'. Even in these Homes, however, matrons would usually make an exception to their general ruling for a couple who were genuinely contemplating marriage, and a number of marriages had taken place from the Homes. Equally, there were exceptions to the other rules too, and in one Home where boy friends could supposedly visit freely, the residents maintained that staff exerted pressure on them to give up boy friends they considered unsuitable. If the staff approved of the boy, all was well, 'but if they don't like 'im, then 'es aht o' t' winder'.

The residents themselves were divided in their attitude to visits from boy friends. There was quite a prevalent feeling that they did not want to be visited either by the putative father or by any other boy friends, and some refused to see them if they came. There was also a suggestion that a ruling against visits from boy friends was reasonable for the sake of the neighbourhood; one could not have 'gangs of lads' turning up at a Home for Unmarried Mothers. The majority of residents, however, even those who themselves had no wish to be visited by any boy friends, thought that the Mother and Baby Home should not rule against their visits, particularly those from the baby's father. It should be up to each girl to decide for herself whether she wished to maintain contact with him. It was wrong, they thought, to enforce a separation on the natural parents while the girls were in the Home; they were there for a long time and during this period the couple might grow apart, and not be able to go back to each other again. Many residents wanted to talk the situation over with their baby's father: 'I think most of the girls here go back to their lads,' one explained, 'and I think they ought to be able to come up here and see you, and then you can get the rest of it sorted out between you.' Even if this were not so, some argued that the putative father had a right to see his child.

It was perhaps surprising to find the putative fathers so firmly excluded from so many Homes in view of the common belief that if the mother was to develop any sense of responsibility towards her child she must spend some time living with her baby. It would be reasonable to assume that if the presence of the child was necessary to the mother, a sight of it might have a salutory effect on the father. Indeed the matrons who encouraged the putative fathers to visit were very sure that this was the case. One told us that some of the fathers were so deeply touched by the sight of the baby, that it had been the making of some marriages.

The different rulings on visits from the baby's father suggest a dichotomy of purpose in the Homes. Those who encourage the putative father to visit and respect his concern for the child show a purpose in line with current practice in social work, hoping that the putative father and the mother together may be helped to work out the problems of their relationship and the future of their baby. In the Homes where the putative father was not allowed to visit, his claim to be concerned for his child's welfare was not entertained. The preoccupation was with his relationship with the mother. Here it seemed there was an affinity of purpose with the early Rescue Homes, and that rules were designed to break off an 'immoral' association. One Chaplain expressed this view by asking, if a girl has no intention of marrying the baby's father, what purpose can there be in allowing him to visit?

The difference in these attitudes to the role of the putative father are to some extent illustrative of the changing view of society as a whole. For centuries English law has refused to recognize any relationship between a natural father and his illegitimate child, and Mother and Baby Homes which deny the putative father any rights or responsibilities for his child do no more than follow what is still largely the legal position. There are signs, however, that public opinion is moving towards a fuller recognition of the natural tie, and lately some rights in the father have been legally acknowledged.[1]

[1] Section 3 of the Legitimacy Act 1959 makes it possible for the natural father to apply for custody and/or access to his illegitimate child.
In the High Court of Justice (Chancery Division) on December 15, 1965 and in the Court of Appeal on February 15, 1966, in the case of 'In re "C" (an infant)', custody of a 17-month old boy was awarded to his natural father against his mother's wishes, and was removed from prospective adopters agreed by the natural mother who had had him for 15 months.
See also 'Fatherless by Law': A study by the Board for Social Responsibility of the National Assembly of the Church of England, 1966, for a discussion of developments in the law relating to the position of natural fathers.

Visiting Hours

All but six Homes which allowed visitors to come at any time had set visiting hours, usually Saturday and Sunday afternoons. Five Homes allowed visiting on one afternoon during the week, but six limited it to Saturday afternoon only. Alternative arrangements for parents who were not able to come at the normal times were not always made willingly. The residents were free in all but two of the Homes to go out with their visitors for the afternoon. Six homes allowed them out before lunch and they could usually stay out until six o'clock or later. If the residents could not or did not wish to go out, visitors could be entertained in the Home for two or three hours.

Two reasons were given for limiting visiting hours. Firstly, matrons generally agreed that it was easier to have all the visitors come at a specified time rather than to answer the door continually throughout the week to occasional callers. Secondly, visiting times were limited for the sake of those who for various reasons had few or no visitors. It was argued that restricted visiting minimized the difference between these residents and those whose families and friends could come often. It seemed to us that neither of these reasons was a valid justification for the policies in force.

In the first place, Homes allowing free visiting were not inundated by an incessant stream of visitors. Friends and relatives of unmarried mothers, like everyone else, have their daily commitments, and week-end afternoons and possibly evenings for some local visitors are by far the most likely times to visit the Mother and Baby Home. Nor did it really seem that the residents with few people to visit them were helped by the limits set on others. It is possible that restrictions have the reverse effect, and simply underline the isolation of the same few residents who are always left alone when the friends and relatives of others are visiting determinedly at every permitted visiting time. There was some evidence, too, that short or infrequent visiting periods actually increased the number of girls with few visitors. When parents could only be with their daughters for two or three hours, those who had little money and had to travel a long way by public transport tended to make the journey only once or twice during their daughter's stay. We were also told that when visiting was permitted fairly freely girls who went out often would sometimes invite one of the others to go with them. The current trend in all residential institutions is for a greater degree of contact between residents and their families, and between the Home and the community. In this respect there is no reason why Mother and Baby Homes should not move with the main stream of social policy, and we felt that many Homes should try to be more generous over visiting hours than they are, not least because many of their residents are very homesick and miss their families greatly.

There are in fact good reasons for encouraging contact between residents and their familes. Illegitimacy is a family problem and the future of the baby and his mother will be at least partly influenced by the attitudes and opinions of the mother's own family. This was not sufficiently recognized in the Homes. It sometimes seemed that matrons placed an unrealistic stress on the need for a resident to make her own uninfluenced decision. As an instance of this one Maternity Home ruled that after parents had visited their daughter immediately following her confinement, they could not visit again for three weeks so that the girl would have time to come to her decision on her own. The rule did not achieve its purpose, as the matron herself admitted, because parents who were determined that their daughters should know their views could always write to her. This ruling caused considerable hardship to the residents in the Home where it applied. They, like other unmarried mothers needed to be in touch with their parents over this time. And parents too surely have a right to express their views. If they are in agreement with their daughter's plans it is senseless to deprive her of their support, and if their wishes are opposed to hers the conflict will not be resolved by keeping them apart.

OTHER RULES

Correspondence

Letters to and from the residents were generally completely free of censorship. Some matrons exercised a degree of surveillance by collecting the post and examining handwriting and postmarks before handing out the letters to the girls. Only one matron told us that she sometimes opened letters, usually just those addressed to approved schoolgirls[1] though she might occasionally open others if she particularly wanted to know something of the background of the girl to whom they were written. Another matron did not open letters but might, if she suspected that a letter came from a married man, or that a resident was receiving money, ask that a letter be opened in her presence and then shown to her. None of the residents seen in either of these Homes

---

[1] According to information supplied by the Home Office, in particular instances there might be some reason why an approved schoolgirl required special consideration in respect of outside contacts, including correspondence. In these cases appropriate arrangements need to be made between the Approved School and the Mother and Baby Home, with the knowledge of the girl and her parents.

had ever had their letters opened, and the only reports of censorship came from two other Homes. In one the printed list of rules stated that all correspondence went through the matron's hands, 'but will not be opened unless she considers it necessary'. Here the residents told us that the staff always opened official letters but personal ones were not censored unless a girl's parents had given their permission. In the other Home the matron denied opening letters. The residents claimed their mail was censored and letters from boy friends were not given to them.

Telephone Calls

In two Homes the residents had a coin-operated phone box for their own use, and a similar installation was planned for two others. Four Homes permitted the residents to use the staff telephone. Because the telephone was usually situated in the office or staff sitting-room this proved a source of annoyance and inconvenience to everyone. Privacy for a conversation was only possible if the staff interrupted what they were doing and left the room. Frustration was increased in two of the Homes where residents could only receive incoming calls during one hour each evening. Ten to twelve residents all hoping for a telephone call within the hour, would resent anyone speaking for more than a few minutes, and parents or friends who had not been able to get through at the proper time annoyed the staff by ringing later when they were not allowed to speak to the residents. The other Homes avoided these problems in a way that seemed to us an unwarrantable limitation on the residents' contact with their families, by prohibiting all but emergency telephone calls. Another problem caused by the lack of access to a telephone was the difficulty residents experienced in contacting their social workers. As we discovered when trying to arrange interviews with them, social workers spend only short and infrequent periods in their office; telephoning them from a public call box could be expensive and was often frustrating.

Smoking

Smoking was forbidden in all the Homes in the nursery for the sake of the babies, and usually in bedrooms as a precaution against fire. Other rules on smoking served to balance the interest of smokers and non-smokers. One of the living-rooms might be reserved for one of the groups; or if one room was used both as a dining-room and a sitting-room, smokers might be asked not to smoke for a period before each meal, or to limit smoking to certain times after meals. In nine Homes the strictness of the rules governing smoking suggested an attack on the habit itself. Smoking was either confined to certain very limited periods or the number of cigarettes that could be smoked in a day were rationed. In one Home residents had to go outside to the laundry if they wanted a cigarette, and in two Homes smoking was completely forbidden. In one of these the matron told the residents that smoking was forbidden for the sake of their health, and to avoid the danger of fire. Her real reasons, she told us, were different: most of the residents were on grants from their local Council, or the National Assistance Board, as it then was. She thought it was wrong that they should spend this money on inessentials. Smoking was not essential to anyone, and the girls should learn to do without it.

THE RESIDENTS' REACTIONS TO THE RULES

The rules and restrictions on personal behaviour to which the residents were subject must have been 'quite alien to the experience of most of those who enter Mother and Baby Homes.'[1] In spite of this, residents accepted the situation without much questioning, acknowledging the need for some rules at least. The Ministry of Health noted a similar apathetic acquiesence in unaccustomed and sometimes stringent rules. Perhaps the explanation for this lies in the general passivity common to many women nearing the end of their pregnancy.[2] Another possible reason may be found in the guilt feelings of unmarried mothers which lead them to expect and perhaps even to welcome curtailment of their liberty as a form of punishment. This attitude was illustrated during a group discussion on the rule forbidding residents to go out in the evening. In one girl's view residents should stay in in the evenings, because 'after all, we ought to suffer something. We've done wrong and we should suffer in some way, and I think it's quite a good thing that we don't go out, at least we're missing something'.

Although the general mood was one of acceptance, the rules provoked other reactions too, and some residents frankly and deliberately broke those they regarded as completely unreasonable. We have already instanced the disregard of rules forbidding residents to bring food into the Home. Similarly they ignored the strictest rules against smoking. They openly admitted to 'smoking on the sly', and sprayed the bedrooms liberally with hair lacquer to mask the evidence of a secret cigarette. As would be expected, complaints about rules arose most often in the most restrictive Homes. The residents complained of

[1] Hall and Howes 1965.
[2] Caplan 1961.

numerous petty and unreasonable rules which made them feel irritable and encaged. They particularly resented situations in which new and different rules were constantly appearing, so that they found themselves in trouble for breaking rules they did not know existed. This led to perpetual feelings of guilty apprehension, so much so in one Home that a newcomer thought she had to ask permission 'to be excused'. One resident stated in her questionnaire: 'The girls I feel would feel better if these Homes were not quite so official, there are too many rules and regulations which are quite unnecessary.' Another wrote politely: 'Please don't have too many rules.' These feelings were recognized and understood by three matrons who deliberately avoided restrictions as far as possible. They explained that expectant mothers nearing the end of their pregnancy could be easily upset; that rules created tensions, and girls who, because of their situation, were feeling bitterness and resentment could be easily goaded into lashing out against restrictions. If tensions could be avoided, they argued, so too could the reactions against them. This was well illustrated by a young girl facing a particularly difficult situation who told us: 'We don't seem to have many rules here. The matron isn't at all strict. She's very easy going. And so we don't bother to break the rules really.'

ENFORCING THE RULES

If rules are worth anything they have to be enforced. The context in which the staff of Mother and Baby Homes have to do this is a very difficult one. First they are dealing with a continually changing population: rules and patterns of behaviour must be constantly re-stated if they are not to be lost or distorted as residents change, and this can give them an undesirable and otherwise unnecessary emphasis. Secondly, short of asking a resident to leave, there are few sanctions that can be applied to those who break the rules. Finally, it is likely that amongst the residents of a Mother and Baby Home there will be some who because of their disturbed condition will demand a greater tolerance than the others. Without careful explanation and tactful handling on the part of the staff, this individual treatment can easily be interpreted by the other residents as favouritism.

We asked the matrons how they acted when residents broke rules, or otherwise created trouble. Simple rule breaking was generally dealt with by restricting the particular privilege of the individual who had abused it—forbidding smoking for a girl who had smoked out of hours, or stopping outings for one who had come back late. Group punishments might occasionally be imposed, but one matron said that she rarely had to act in this way because the residents 'sorted themselves out'. As an illustration she told us how she discovered that someone had been smoking at a forbidden hour in a forbidden place; the offender refused to own up so the matron announced that smoking for all residents would be forbidden. Within half an hour the girl responsible had come to her because 'the others had threatened her with murder and goodness what'.

In discussing discipline matrons stressed that they were dealing with girls whose physical and psychological conditions made them unreasonably touchy. Tact and tolerance soothed many irritations. They were qualities needed by all the staff, and one matron told us that the doctor had remarked on the sudden drop in the number of girls with raised blood pressure which coincided with the departure of a particular member of staff. These matrons hoped to avoid direct confrontation over rules, and evolved schemes to keep the peace by other means. One had a suggestions box into which residents could post anonymous questions or suggestions about the running of the Home. Each week the box was opened and the matron discussed the contents with the residents. Another held what the residents called 'complaints day'. After prayers each Monday morning, the matron announced any special happenings during the week, and made this an opportunity to talk over with the residents the things that were going wrong in the Home.

INFLUENCES ON THE RULES

All the matrons told us that they tried to keep rules and restrictions to a minimum, but we found, like the Ministry of Health that 'some matrons use more rules and apply regulations with less tolerance than others'. There were no obvious reasons why this should be so. The Homes were not always uniformly restrictive or permissive, and a stringent rule on one subject might be accompanied by a liberal policy on another. Factors which might have been expected to influence the number or type of rules, such as the size of the Home, the authority providing it, or the type of residents admitted did not in fact have a marked effect. The key factor appeared to be the personality of the matron; whether she liked to work within a strict or relaxed situation was the basic issue.

Other factors did exercise some influence on the tenor of the rules. The approach to religion was one. The two Homes where rules were most numerous and most restrictive were also those in which an evangelical approach was most evident. There was also some evidence that staff who were badly over-worked tended to react with attempts to regulate the conduct of the residents and the routine of the Home, understandably feeling perhaps that their work might be eased if everything proceeded according to a strictly defined pattern. Habit was another influence on the pattern of life. Rules and routines assumed an independence of the situation for which they had originally been created, and were carried on after the initial need had changed or even disappeared. Two matrons admitted during the interviews that they unthinkingly operated certain rules and routines which on reflection were neither relevant nor necessary. Closely allied with habit is the restrictive tradition of residential care for unmarried mothers. By modern standards rules forbidding the use of make-up, reserving the right to inspect residents' belongings, or claiming the need to censor correspondence, may appear as an intolerable interference with personal liberty and privacy. Yet to matrons who have worked for twenty years or more in this service, modern Homes must seem models of freedom. As recently as 1946, a study of services for unmarried mothers[1] described some Mother and Baby Homes as 'extremely old fashioned . . . [they] have locked doors, open all letters, and remove pocket money and note paper, [they] are virtually prisons and the more self-respecting girls would not want to enter them even if they needed them badly'. Finally, it seemed that rules were created in response to crises. One Home introduced a rule that all residents must return to the Home by 6.30 p.m. after a group had created a disturbance in the town. Two others prevented mothers from pushing their babies out in prams following incidents when residents had left their babies unsupervised in parks. Restrictive reactions in such situations may be quite understandable, but it would be a pity to legislate always with the most irresponsible residents in mind. All potential hazards cannot possibly be anticipated and Homes should be able to withstand the occasional crises which must inevitably occur.

No general rules for Mother and Baby Homes can be stipulated. Of necessity individual Homes will have different rules; the routine and pattern must be suited to the residents admitted. Restrictions which would be quite unsuitable for older women used to an independent life will be essential for schoolgirls who need the discipline and support of a more structured situation. For this reason, Homes might find it easier to devise appropriate rules and routines if they limited their

[1] P. E. P. 1946.

intake to particular age-groups, rather than admitting all ages as the majority do at present. Within the limits of the different Homes, the aim should be to preserve the independence of the residents and allow as much freedom as possible. Following the recommendation of the study quoted above, as a general policy, 'the commonsense rules of behaviour necessary in any community should be the only rules imposed'.

9

RELATIONSHIPS IN THE HOMES

The most profound and yet the most subtle influence on the residents during their stay in a Mother and Baby Home are the personal relationships they experience there. In this chapter we consider the relationships in the Homes and some of the factors which bear on them.

THE RESIDENTS AND THE STAFF

The Residents and the Matron
In every Home the most important relationship was that between the residents and the matron. The matron's influence, continually apparent during the interviews with the residents, was also remarked on by the social workers interviewed. Repeatedly they judged the quality of a Home by the matron. We heard of matrons who made happy Homes out of the worst conditions, of others who soured the atmosphere of the best, and of striking changes in the quality of care following a change of matron.

Many residents found their matron a real mother figure. 'She's just like a second mother to us really, isn't she?' was a typical comment. Matrons who came into the residents' sitting-room and watched their television, or had a 'right good laff' with them or helped the schoolgirls with their homework, were very different from the impersonal figure of authority many residents had expected. These people were 'not like a matron' at all, they were 'just like your Mam'.

Helping the residents with the personal problems of their illegitimate pregnancy, the matrons considered, was a major part of their job, and in about a third of the Homes the residents appeared to gain from the matron real sympathy and firm support. They could take their worries to her and she would 'really get down to things' and talk them over, ('You can say anything to her, she's terribly understanding') and the girls would feel much better. Naturally enough, not all the matrons were so approachable. One was said to 'queen it' and going to see her was 'like going into the headmaster's study'. It never occurred to some residents to talk over their plans and problems with their matron. Sometimes they were aware that the matron was willing to help them. Yet they hesitated: 'I don't know. I would feel awfully silly if I went to see ...' was one rather embarrassed confession. 'There's too much of a gulf between us' explained a girl from another Home. 'I think it's the age really.'

Six matrons were really disliked and even feared. During a group interview one girl saw her mother coming up the drive, but she was hesitant about going out to see her because 'it'll be alright now, she'll [matron] be nice to me while my mother's here and while you're here, but as soon as you've both gone I might get into trouble and I just daren't go'. Four matrons were said to be two-faced like this, charming when visitors, relatives or social workers were there—sarcastic, vindictive, inconsistent and unpredictable on their own: 'She's always flying off the handle' said one resident, and another joked 'she's never on the handle'. Two matrons were accused of deliberately trying to upset the girls. Another nagged. Another openly went through the residents' belongings and read letters that were left around. Two were said to be constantly reminding the residents of the reason for their stay in the Home. This, the residents found hard to bear: 'They think we don't realize that we've done wrong, but we do. We know and we want to forget and we don't need it rubbed into us all the time.' And from another Home: 'After all, anyone can make a mistake, and we have our punishment just through carrying the baby, they don't need to keep rubbing it in all the time and making us feel worse'. Usually the members of the group appeared to be united in their attitude to the matron, but occasionally there was a resident who went against the general opinion. Some could not get on with matrons who were generally liked. Equally, individual residents found kindness and understanding in unpopular matrons, one of whom was described by a resident as 'a wonderful matron, strict to a point, but kind at heart and very sincere in any way she can help a mother-to-be and a baby'.

Any relationship has two sides, and the matrons expressed their views of the residents. Some found them co-operative and easy to deal with. Three matrons who were particularly hard-pressed said that the residents knew this and responded with kindness and consideration, and the Mother Superior of a Home run by nuns said she was continually amazed at the contentment the residents displayed in such secluded surroundings. (Though she admitted to wondering whether this serenity would last if they had to stay much longer!) Other matrons had their troubles. Their patience was tried by residents described as 'thoughtless', 'feckless', 'untidy' and 'irresponsible'. Here again there were frequent exceptions, and the strong influence of individuals was mentioned. One co-operative girl could lift the spirit of a place; a single trouble-maker dragged it down. We were also told that easy and difficult residents tended to come in batches, so that with the continually changing population of a Mother and Baby Home, the whole atmosphere of a Home could change dramatically in a few weeks.

Residents and Other Staff
By contrast with the matron, the residents' relationships with assistant staff were less strong, even though assistants might have as much or more daily contact with residents than the matron had. Possibly this was because the matron was the figure of authority for staff and residents alike. Whatever the reason, relations with assistant staff played a small part in the group interviews. They were mentioned; some nagged and harped on the girls' sins, others were sympathetic and good fun. Occasionally an individual revealed a strikingly good or strikingly bad relationship with one of the assistant staff, which to her personally seemed to mean more than the contact with the matron, but this was rare.

RELATIONSHIPS AMONGST THE RESIDENTS

If the thought of going into a Mother and Baby Home had frightened most residents, so too did the prospect of living with a lot of other unmarried mothers. 'I thought there'd be a lot of tarts in here', said one girl, and another had seen herself living amongst 'a whole lot of streetwalkers'. The public image of the unmarried mother as a hard, fast little piece who 'has had a good run for her money' is seldom a true one, and it was a welcome discovery to find on arrival that the other residents were ordinary girls like themselves, just as worried and just as unhappy.

Before they came into the Home, it seemed that almost every resident we saw had imagined that she was the only one ever to face an illegitimate pregnancy. She felt quite alone, guilty and conspicuous, thinking that everyone must be whispering about her behind her back. Coming into the Home marked the end of this loneliness. The relief of being amongst others who shared the same overwhelming problems was enormous. 'You can relax'; this was said over and over again. Residents were no longer frightened of finding people staring at them.

They could begin to take life calmly and start to think things out. 'You can sleep again at night', and for the first time many of them could 'forget the horror of it' and begin 'to accept the pregnancy naturally'.

This feeling of relief was tempered in the beginning at least by the difficulty of settling into the Home. Few girls were used to group living, and they felt lonely and uncertain amongst so many strangers. Many missed their families quite desperately, especially at first. All the groups raised the problem of homesickness, and we saw it in many of the newcomers who had only been in the Home a day or two. The residents thought this initial period of homesickness was inevitable. There was nothing anyone could do to lessen it; it was something that everyone had to cope with alone. Its duration depended partly on each individual girl, and partly on the tradition in the Home. In two or three Homes we were told that each newcomer had to face a barrage of personal and embarrassing questions before being accepted into the group. Others said that no one spoke to them at all at first, and they thought 'Oh goodness, is it going to be like this all the time?' In some Homes, though, the residents were said to be very kind and friendly; as one explained 'You feel here that you are all in the same boat and you do all you can to help each other.'

There were a few residents who never really settled down. To some, living with other unmarried mothers only intensified their problems and underlined the difficulties they were trying to forget. In four Homes, a general feeling of uneasiness seemed to be due to a bad relationship with the matron. These exceptions apart, once the residents had overcome their homesickness, and grown used to living with so many other people, they realized the benefits of companionship. They found relief in shared problems and real sympathy amongst others who knew the same feelings. The groups often mentioned the support they received from one another. In one Maternity Home the residents described how they went rushing upstairs to see each newly delivered baby, and one said that the pleasure on the faces of the other girls 'seems to give you a lot of strength'. Living together could be fun as well as comforting. The burden of hiding a secret fell away. Family tensions were forgotten. The residents relaxed, and found to their surprise that 'We're always laughing here, in spite of all this.'

Most groups admitted that there was friction from time to time, or that some residents were at odds with the rest. They thought this was inevitable; it was difficult for a lot of unhappy people to live together. Everyone had to watch their step and be careful what they said. People were so easily offended. Several residents acknowledged the touchiness, the quick jumpy reaction, and the flash of temper that the matrons had mentioned. Like the matrons, they too explained it as an effect of their condition. One girl admitted that she had gone up to her room one night and cried and cried. It was only temper and she knew she was being silly, but she could not pull herself together. Tempers flared sometimes. There were hard feelings and arguments, and in one Home, fighting was not far away; 'but you can't bash somebody with a lump, can you?' 'So you say—just you wait till you've lost your lump and then I'll get you, but by the time she's lost it you've forgotten all about it'. There were also occasional stories of cattiness and hostility directed towards one particular resident. In spite of these admitted difficulties many residents said that they were happier than they had ever thought it possible to be in such a situation, and that they would miss the companionship of the other residents when they left. Leaving the Home was in fact often dreaded as much as coming into it. 'Everyone cries when they come in,' they told us, 'but they cry when they go out too.'

INFLUENCES ON RELATIONSHIPS

Personal Qualities of Staff

In considering the factors influencing relationships between the staff and the residents, the first and most obvious is the personal qualities of the staff. The Williams Committee concluded that all the qualities needed by residential staff could only be found in 'a phalanx of archangels'. Certainly the job demands 'great qualities of heart and mind and skills of a high order'. The hours are long, there is the constant strain of close contact with unhappy people, many Homes are understaffed, and the working conditions in most are bad. Over and above these difficulties the matron has the burden of responsibility for staff and residents. She has to supervise the work of the staff; to maintain harmony amongst residents of different ages, different levels of intelligence and different backgrounds; and on occasions 'act as a buffer' between residents and staff.

Few matrons and even fewer assistant staff had specific training designed to help them with the problems they encountered, and when they succeeded in establishing a good relationship with the residents it was largely due to their own personal qualities. Amongst the qualities shared by the matrons and staff with whom residents seemed able to make a good relationship were a genuine understanding and liking for the residents, a sense of humour, the capacity to evoke respect, and an ability to comfort. As has been indicated, however, relationships were not always good. When residents admitted an inability to communicate their feelings to the staff, the reasons they most frequently suggested for this were the age-gap and the fact that so many of the staff had never been married. Older unmarried staff, the residents felt, could not be expected to understand their feelings. It was taken for granted that young married women, preferably with children of their own, would come closer to appreciating the agony of deciding the baby's future and the pain of parting for adoption. On a more practical level they would also know what it was like to be pregnant. 'Anyway she's married and she's much more understanding' was typical of the references to the married women who worked in the Homes. Many of them had families of their own. The girls would give them their confidences and there would be 'great confabs over coffee'.

Youth and marriage, however, did not automatically ensure success. Of the few young staff we saw, one was thoroughly unpopular. She was said to have 'all her degrees and everything', but in practice 'she doesn't know which end of a baby to hold'. Nor was marriage a guarantee of understanding. Although two of the four married matrons were considered by the residents to be most understanding, the other two were regarded as unapproachable. In our view the most relevant factor in the quality of the relationship established was whether the staff had a knowledge of the world the girls lived in, and an insight into their attitudes. We met staff who were both ignorant and frankly impatient of modern youth. They admitted that they could neither understand nor communicate with the girls who came into the Homes. Equally, their own attitudes were unintelligible to the residents. One social worker explained the impasse by the fact that staff who had worked in Mother and Baby Homes for years simply did not realize how conditions had changed; though the staff were kind and well-intentioned, to the residents, their attitudes appeared rigid and old-fashioned.

The danger of staff losing contact with the normal community is a potential hazard in all residential Homes,[1] but it must be particularly great in Mother and Baby Homes where acute staff shortages result in the loss of free time[2] and inadequate accommodation makes entertaining friends in the Home impossible. It is widely recognized that residents in Homes may become 'institutionalized' through lack of

[1] Williams 1967, Miller 1966.
[2] See Chapter 10.

outside contacts. It is not so readily acknowledged that staff may suffer a similar condition, and organizations providing Homes should regard it as a duty to give their staff the time and opportunity to maintain their contacts with the normal community.

Size of Home and Type of Residents Admitted
Two factors which the staff mentioned as influencing relationships were the size of the Home and the type of residents admitted. Evidence on the effect of both factors was conflicting. As regards the size of the Home, one school of thought preferred small Homes. When the staff lived closely with the residents, it was felt that harmony was easily maintained; difficulties could be anticipated before they erupted into real trouble. At any sign of unrest, tactful enquiries, and possibly room changes, might be all that was necessary. On the other hand, it was argued that the close living in the small Homes was a source of friction. Not only did the girls become irritated with one another, but the constant contact with the residents eventually snapped the patience of the staff.

From the residents' point of view, it seemed to us that the advantages lay with the small Homes of less than ten residents. Here it appeared that residents lived as a single united group, the routine of the Home was informal, and individual tastes and idiosyncracies were respected. We also noted positive attributes in the Homes with more than twenty beds. In Homes of this size, routine and rules were obviously necessary, and therefore more acceptable to the residents than in the small Homes. There were enough residents for friendship groups to be selective, and sufficient staff to make it likely that a resident would find someone with whom she could form a good relationship. The least satisfactory size of Home, in terms of the residents' happiness, was around 15 to 16 beds. Homes of this size lacked the favourable aspects of the larger and the smaller ones. The residents in them tended to split into two groups; mothers and expectant mothers, and there was often some hostility between the two. When it comes to planning new Homes, the residents' happiness will be only one consideration; economic and staffing problems must also be taken into account and it may be that these different factors are not entirely compatible. The best size of Home must still be considered open to question.

Similarly we felt that there was a need for more thought to be given to the admission policy of Homes. As we have seen nearly all Homes have some criteria of eligibility, but in spite of this most do admit a very wide range of residents. This suited some matrons. They told us that the older women mothered the younger girls, and that both were helped by this. They saw mutual benefit, too, when residents who had had an easy life saw the difficulties that others had to contend with, and when those with difficult backgrounds realized that they were not the only ones 'to get into trouble'. These are the advantages of a mixed intake which should be acknowledged. Against these must be set the difficulties, already noted, of planning routines and fixing rules in non-selective Homes. Of greater importance was the impression received from the group interviews, that individual residents drew most support from the group and were most relaxed with one another when the group was a relatively homogenous one. It seemed also that the maintenance of order was simplified in these Homes.

The Status of the Residents

The manner in which order is maintained is itself an influence on the nature of the relationships which can develop in the Homes. The more formal the rules and their enforcement, the less personal can be the relations between the residents who must obey the rules and the staff who uphold them. This brings us to a consideration of the status of the residents mentioned at the beginning of chapter seven and foreshadowed in the first chapter in the difficulty of finding a term to describe the unmarried mothers living in the Homes.

The status of unmarried mothers in Mother and Baby Homes is very hard to define. Although we have called them 'residents', they do not have the status of other sorts of 'residents'; for example, those living in a hotel, a boarding house or a residential job. The degree of personal freedom and individuality permitted to an unmarried mother in a Mother and Baby Home, does not bear comparison with that any of the other 'residents' would be entitled to expect. Before going into a Mother and Baby Home, unmarried mothers may be described by their social workers as 'clients'. Once in the Home they lose the client status of choosing to make use of a service according to their own particular need. They become instead the recipient of a fixed and pre-determined type of service which they have no choice but to accept. Perhaps the most apt term to suggest their status while in the Home is 'girl', the word used by the staff of the Homes and the social workers. 'Girl' conveys the denial of adult status and responsibility, and the expectations of conformity and obedience to a regulated pattern of life, and yet allows the kindness of approach, the personal and even affectionate interest which were evident on the part of the staff.

The question of status is an important one in relation to the purpose of the Homes. The status accorded to the residents is intimately bound up with the type of service the Homes can provide. Each limits and is limited by the other. We asked the matrons what they were trying to achieve in running the Homes. Nearly always the answer came back in some form or other—to live as a family. Four Homes succeeded in their aim to a remarkable degree. The residents in them repeated over and over again during the interviews 'Well, it's just like a family really', 'It's just like being at home', and questionnaires from these Homes produced such remarks as 'This Home is very well run and the girls are treated more like a family. If all Homes were like this I don't think there would be any complaints.' But the family analogy has its danger. Life in a Mother and Baby Home cannot be exactly like that of a family. The staff must retain a degree of authority and the rules and routine must have a formality which is ultimately incompatible with the family image. When the family life was stressed too much residents were quick to recognize the flaws in the image; to point to the oddities of a family in which only certain members (i.e. the staff) could answer the door; and to remark sarcastically that although staff and residents sat round the table together for 'family meals', the staff had special crockery and sometimes different food.

Yet it is possible to see why the Homes use the image of a family. 'Family Life' conveys a sense of informality and of individuals living in a secure group offering mutual respect, consideration and support. The Homes might come nearer to achieving their objective if they abandoned the total image, and tried instead to identify the separate functions within it which are appropriate to their work.

10

STAFFING

'In residential care, the staff *is* the service.'[1] The type of service that Mother and Baby Homes can offer will depend more on the number and quality of staff they are able to attract, than on any other single factor. If they now provide a service short of their potential, it is partly due to the extreme gravity of the staffing situation, apparent in this chapter.

THE MATRONS

As we have seen the matron was the central figure in every Home. In five Homes she was the only resident member of staff and in three the only full-time member. In spite of her dominant influence, there was no general agreement on her role. When asked what they did, matrons mentioned in reply everything connected with the running of a Mother and Baby Home, from baby care, record keeping, washing and cooking, to painting and decorating and chopping wood. From their replies it was possible to identify several aspects of the matrons' work: they undertook the daily administration of the Home within the limits set by individual management committees; they supervised the housekeeping; and they were responsible for the welfare of their residents, giving them advice and help on their personal problems. These three roles were common to all matrons. In addition others might be concerned with the residents' spiritual welfare, with nursing and baby care, and with teaching mother-craft, personal hygiene, simple housekeeping, or more vaguely 'things that would be useful later on in life'. Yet another aspect of the matrons' work was the need to stand in for any absent member of staff and to do any job that nobody else wished to do. As they themselves told us, the matrons had to be 'Jacks of all trades'; one described her function as 'general dogsbody'.

[1] Huws Jones 1966.

G

In addition to their residential work, matrons in Homes run by Church of England Moral Welfare Organizations might also undertake social work in the community. This arrangement is an inheritance from the early days of moral welfare work, when 'outdoor work' as it was called, was done from Rescue Homes and Shelters by the resident staff. As the work developed separate workers began to be appointed to 'indoor' and 'outdoor' posts, but some remnants of the old system persist; two matrons were the outdoor workers for their area and six others either assisted an outdoor worker when she was pressed, or helped their own residents to find jobs and somewhere to live after leaving the Home.

Most matrons had been working in this field for many years. Only eight had been in their post for less than three years, and four, including one who had been in charge of her Home for twenty-seven years, had been there more than ten years. Before taking their present posts six matrons had worked as assistants in the same Home for periods ranging from two to twenty-five years.

OTHER STAFF

All the Homes had at least one member of staff in addition to the matron. Their functions were not easy to define because the sharing of the work-load varied so much with the size of the Home and the staff establishment. The member of staff next in seniority to the matron was variously described as assistant matron, house matron, or housekeeper. Her duties were often domestic, but she might be expected to assist the matron with administration and welfare work. Generally speaking, in the large Homes, or those that were well staffed, other assistant staff tended to have specific jobs: housekeeper—midwife—laundress—nursery nurse—secretary—cook—and so on. In the others, it was very much a case of everyone co-operating to get things done. Usually senior assistants worked full time and lived in the Home. Non-resident staff were mainly part-time domestic workers, gardeners and night attendants. Without exception this was the case in the south, but in the north nine of the non-resident staff had nursing qualifications and five of the assistant matrons and housekeepers came to the Home daily.

QUALIFICATIONS AND STAFF ESTABLISHMENT

In sixteen Homes at least one member of staff held a nursing qualification, and in nine there were staff with moral welfare qualifications.[1] In three of these Homes there were staff with both qualifications.

The best staffed Homes were the Maternity Homes and those run by the local health authorities. The proportion of qualified staff in these Homes was higher than average; none of the Maternity Homes had less than two resident midwives and there were staff with midwifery and nursing qualifications in each of the local health authority Homes. These Homes were also relatively well supplied with secretarial, domestic, catering and gardening staff. One local health authority Home even had a man coming round to wind the clocks.

Amongst the other Homes there was no common pattern. The staff establishment was not necessarily related to the size of the Home: one Home with eight beds had an establishment of two full-time resident staff and a part-time cook, nurse, domestic help and gardener. Another Home with nineteen beds allowed for three full-time resident staff and a part-time cook. In a third Home with eleven beds the establishment consisted of two resident staff and no other help at all. The Williams Committee noted a similar lack of relationship between size of Home and staff establishment, and suggested that it was due to the failure of management committees to appreciate the nature and amount of work involved in residential care. If this is so, it may be that the fault lies partly with the staff who fail to acquaint their committees with the situation. Nine matrons complained that their staff establishment was inadequate: three said they needed an extra resident member of staff; three wanted gardeners; three help with laundry or domestic work; two secretarial help; one somebody to do the accounts; and one a handyman. Even this is probably an understatement of the seriousness of the situation, for it seemed to us that some of the staff had grown used to their enormous burden of work. In nearly half the Homes there was no domestic help; a third had no cook; a similar proportion lacked gardeners; secretarial help was available in only five Homes and most of the other Homes only had these forms of help part-time. Only seven Homes had night staff and in the others a resident member of the staff had to be on call. In Homes full of new babies and expectant mothers nearing the end of their pregnancy broken nights were an expected hazard, and an additional strain on staff already working to the limit of their capacity. The burden must be particularly great in the twelve Homes which had no night assistants and only one or two resident

[1] The words 'moral welfare' are used here as a general term describing the special training in social work given by organizations of the Church of England, the Methodist Church and the Salvation Army.

staff. In one of these the matron had been called during the night before our visit to take an expectant mother to hospital sixteen miles away, yet she had to be on duty again first thing next morning.

SHORTAGE OF STAFF

In common with other residential Homes, Mother and Baby Homes experience acute difficulty in recruiting staff, especially resident staff. To find anyone to live in was hard enough. To get someone who was particularly suitable for the work in a Mother and Baby Home, with its long hours and heavy emotional demands, and who could settle down happily with existing staff, was practically impossible. Ten Homes out of 23 had a vacant residential post when we visited them. Some had been advertising unsuccessfully for months. Lack of suitable applicants meant either that the post was filled by someone who was recognized from the beginning as unsuitable, or that it remained empty. The former course of action resulted in appointments that were short lived and disastrous. The latter led to almost intolerable pressure on the remaining staff. One matron, who was the only resident staff in a Home for ten residents and who had only part-time assistance and domestic help, had resigned several months before our visit because she felt unable to carry on with so little help. A new matron was appointed, and concluded within a fortnight that she could not manage either. The previous matron returned temporarily until a replacement could be found, and when we interviewed her, she had not had a holiday for six months, nor even a day off for three weeks. She told us she was just so tired, she could sit down and cry. The strains and stresses of residential work make it imperative that staff should have time to relax and refresh themselves, yet staff shortages were such that we were told that it was often impossible for matrons and their assistants to take their full allowance of off-duty time. Some could not even take their annual leave. When one matron was asked how much free time she was supposed to have, she replied: 'Supposed to have! I'm glad you said *supposed* to have.' She had not had her full allowance of leave once in fourteen years. Most Homes hoped to be able to arrange relief staff when resident staff were on holiday. But one or two matrons had found that temporary staff were more of a hindrance than a help, and refused to have them. In these Homes, and in those which could not get relief workers, the staff either shared out the extra work caused by an absent colleague, or went without their holiday. One Home was sometimes closed for a month so that the staff could go on leave.

THE STAFFING CRISIS

The staffing crisis in Mother and Baby Homes is not unique; all types of residential institutions face situations of similar gravity. The reasons for them were examined by the Williams Committee and amongst ways of alleviating the difficulties the Committee recommend improvements in salaries,[1] hours of work, working conditions, and training leading to an enhanced status. Although each one of these is important, it seemed to us that two other factors should be singled out for special stress in the case of Mother and Baby Homes.

The first is allied to the failure of management committees (and, as the Williams Committee also points out, the failure of the general public) to appreciate the nature of residential work. It seemed that in the case of Mother and Baby Homes this was part of a more fundamental failure to think out the purpose of the Homes. Many were staffed as though their only purpose was to provide accommodation at its most basic level of food and shelter. Few of the staff in the service would be content with this as their sole aim. They would see helping the residents through their social and emotional difficulties as an intrinsic element of their work, and to this the Homes with religious associations would add concern for the residents' spiritual well-being. Yet matrons had no time to do what they felt was their real work; the burden of mundane household chores and routine administration was too great. The residents recognized the pressures under which the matrons worked. They told us often that they would have liked to talk things over with the matron, but that they did not like to bother her when they knew she had so much to do. Matrons in their turn were aware of this, and though they appreciated the consideration which led residents to leave them undisturbed when at last they had time to sit down, they were conscious that they were failing them and they felt guilty. As one matron said, such a situation 'shouldn't be allowed to happen when you're dealing with human beings'.

If Mother and Baby Homes are to offer their residents a service of

---

[1] We were unsuccessful in attempting to discover what salaries staff were earning, though usually we were able to find out what salary scales were in operation. All the local health authority Homes and two voluntary Homes paid their qualified nursing staff according to the Whitley Scale. Salvation Army officers and the Methodist deaconess received allowances fixed by their headquarters, and nuns received no payment. Other Homes paid salaries according to a scale laid down by the diocese, or by a Home's committee of management. Twice we were told that a committee could not afford salary scales as high as the Whitley Scale and twice that when funds were running low, the scale of the Home itself could not be paid in full. One matron saw low salaries as an advantage, because it ensured that the staff worked not for financial interest but through concern 'for the life and souls of those who God sends here'.

support, staffing requirements must be geared to such a purpose. The matron should not be a 'general dogsbody'. She should work with the residents, while other staff should do the cooking, cleaning, gardening and secretarial work. Committee members are not the only ones who may have to be convinced of this. Some matrons themselves were unwilling to delegate any aspect of their work. Three matrons would not have secretarial help because they considered the work too confidential to be entrusted to a secretary. Others did not want domestic help because they felt that residents were more likely to confide in them if they were working together round the house, than if the matron had to be approached in her room. There may be some truth in this, but the matron who helps in the kitchen or laundry because that is how she can best help the residents is working in a very different situation from the one who is cooking the lunch because there will not be any unless she does.

Secondly, a reconsideration of the manner of staffing residential Homes is urgently needed. The insistence that all senior staff should be resident must be abandoned. The view is still advanced that non-resident staff do not fit into the life of a Mother and Baby Home. It is said that they destroy the sense of community and that daily staff, who return to their own families each evening, cannot establish the close intimate relationship with unmarried mothers that make the resident staff such a profound influence on the girls. Three matrons who took this view chose to work short staffed until a vacant resident post could be filled even when daily help was available.

There is now such a shortage of resident staff, in every kind of institution, that it is no longer realistic to imagine that the traditional method of staffing Homes with resident single women can continue. To some it may remain the ideal, but in present circumstances the chances of achieving it are remote. The real choice is not between resident or non-resident staff, but between employing non-resident staff or allowing the existing staff to work under strength for months at a time, and this is far from ideal. Inevitably, after a time, when staff have to carry an extra burden in addition to their normal heavy work load, something must suffer. It can only be the care of the residents or the health of the staff, and to our knowledge two matrons had been seriously ill in the past year. Some Homes had already abandoned the traditional patterns and evolved new solutions. In one, a widowed matron lived with her son in a house across the road from the Mother and Baby Home. Two night assistants slept in the Home by turn, and the matron could be called if necessary by internal telephone. In another Home, the matron was the only permanent resident, and her assistant staff worked a rota for sleeping in the Home. In a third Home a married woman was employed and she lived in the Home with her husband. These three Homes were in the north. So, too, were the other Homes in which assistant staff at all levels of seniority were employed successfully on a daily or even a part-time basis, and there was nothing to suggest that the quality of care in this region was lower than that in the south.

There are positive advantages in the employment of non-resident staff and these should be set against any possible loss in the sense of community. Staff who come to the Home daily can lessen the isolation of an otherwise completely residential institution. Equally they can take an understanding of the problems of illegitimate maternity to the community. Many of the non-resident staff employed in the Homes visited were married women with children of their own, and far from this being a handicap in their contact with the residents, it was apparent that they often achieved a good relationship with them. Simply because they returned to their own homes and families each day, the residents regarded them as a link with normal life. And because of their own children, they 'understood'. The Williams Committee concluded that one member of the staff in every Home should be resident. This was not a unanimous conclusion; some members of the committee held that there was no need for any member of staff to live in the Home permanently. Such an idea is revolutionary, but if Homes are to recruit the staff they need there must be a revolutionary approach to the problem.

SOURCES OF HELP

There are sources of help potentially available to understaffed Homes and even where overwork is not a serious problem, the same sources may offer valuable support to the staff and form a vital link between Home and community.

Committees
All the Homes, except those run by the Salvation Army and the Roman Catholic nuns, were provided by committees which were themselves responsible for the control and management of the Homes, and these committees formed one possible source of help. In general however committee members did not play an active part in the day-to-day life of the Homes. They did have some contact with the Homes in between

meetings either by visiting on a rota basis, or through regular visits paid by the treasurer or one of the other officers to deal with business or financial matters. Practical help was sometimes given by individual committee members who might organize a handicraft class, visit mothers in hospital or drive them to the adoption society. Otherwise committee members had very little contact with the residents, either because they did not see this as part of their function or because the matron considered it unwise. One matron had discouraged any meetings with the residents following an incident in which a committee member discovered that her brother lived in the same village as one of the mothers, asked the girl her name, and told her that the brother would be so interested to hear where she was. Committee members could, however, provide support of a high quality. This was illustrated during one of our visits when a committee secretary called to see the matron. Together they talked over various problems, the secretary responding sympathetically, knowledgeably and constructively. When she stayed to lunch it was at once apparent from the easy, friendly chat she exchanged with the residents, that she was well-known to everyone and that her interest was appreciated.

We asked the matrons whether or not they found their committees helpful. Eleven replied that their committees 'couldn't be better', and described them as 'first class' and 'extraordinarily good'. They were practical, helpful and understanding. Matrons could take their problems to the committee and rely on receiving a sympathetic hearing, and moral and practical support. Others described their committee members as 'nice' people who 'don't interfere', but added that although the members were willing to help, they had little idea of the practical problems facing the staff. A few matrons were outspoken in their criticism of committees who 'make a nuisance of themselves' and 'just sit and argue'. We were told that they were 'old fashioned', 'out of touch', and 'ill informed', and one matron thought it was time for 'a real shake-up' of the committee system.

Visiting Staff and Voluntary Workers
The burden of work in some Homes was eased by visiting staff and voluntary workers. Both are sources of help which could be used more fully than at present. Few Homes took advantage of facilities offered by the Health or Education Departments of local authorities. Two Homes for young mothers had teachers provided by the local education authority for residents under school leaving age, or in full time education. Two others had handicraft teachers, and a third had

approached the local education authority with a view to starting classes of some sort. About half the matrons said they would contact a health visitor if need arose, but there was little evidence that either this or other local health authority midwifery or nursing services were used regularly.

On the value of voluntary helpers, matrons were divided. Some considered them to be more trouble than they were worth; they threatened the privacy of the residents, and it was rarely possible to find them something suitable to do. Other matrons had no such reservations and found the practical help of voluntary workers invaluable. Voluntary helpers might come in to do the ironing, look after the babies during a film show, or sit in while the matron went out. Others invited residents to their own home for the evening, took them for outings, and visited them in hospital or drove them to the adoption society. Like daily staff, voluntary workers can increase the two-way exchange between the Home and community. Providing always that they are able to appreciate the nature of the work being done in the Home, and that they are willing to accept direction from the matron or the management committee, it would seem that they could make a valuable contribution to the service. In this respect the report of the current enquiry[1] into the role and value of voluntary workers, may offer valuable guidance.

---

[1] The Committee of Enquiry (the Aves Committee) set up jointly by the National Council of Social Service and the National Institute for Social Work Training to examine the role of volunteers, their relationship to professional workers, and the need for training and preparation.

11

MEDICAL CARE

So far we have been concerned mainly with subjects common to most residential Homes. Now we turn to the specialist care provided by Mother and Baby Homes. The particular aspects of care to be considered in the following chapters are specifically connected with unmarried mothers. Consequently the conflicting attitudes towards them and towards Mother and Baby Homes, the ignorance surrounding the problems of illegitimacy and ambiguous maternity, and the uncertainty of purpose in the Homes themselves, are clearly seen.

GENERAL MEDICAL CARE

The residents of Mother and Baby Homes largely use the same general maternity services as married women. Although the Health Services recognize no distinction on the basis of marital status, the unmarried mother, in her own eyes, and sometimes also in the eyes of hospital staff and other patients, carries a distinguishing label.

The routine supervision of the health of the residents and their babies was undertaken by general practitioners with whom the girls registered temporarily. All but four Homes had their own doctor or group of doctors who called regularly at the Home. When residents were seriously ill, or if skilled nursing was required, the patient would be transferred to hospital, but all the Homes were prepared to look after girls who were confined to bed for rest, or any mild illness, and patients could usually be isolated if necessary. Three matrons said that many expectant mothers were in poor health when they first came to the Home, and needed a few days in bed to recover.

Little use was made in the Homes of either dental or psychiatric services. The survey undertaken by the Ministry of Health suggested that arrangements for dental care did not always receive 'the attention due to this important aspect of ante-natal care'. Only one of the Homes we visited expected all residents to make a routine visit to the dentist during their stay. Otherwise it was left to the girls to arrange their own appointments as necessary. Psychiatric treatment, like other specialist facilities, was available to the Homes, but there seemed to be a certain reluctance to use it. One matron said she did not 'go rushing to psychiatrists'. Another frankly admitted that she disapproved of psychiatric treatment, though she conceded that the psychiatrist available to the Home at the time was very good; he was well able to distinguish the 'genuine cases' from 'those that are swinging the lead'. Even when there was no evidence of such attitudes we were told that referrals for psychiatric treatment were rarely necessary.

Yet illegitimacy is commonly regarded as a possible symptom of emotional disturbance.[1] 15 per cent of the unmarried mothers studied by Yelloly were classified as being emotionally disturbed or having considerable psychological problems. Such conditions must exist amongst the unmarried mothers in Mother and Baby Homes and our evidence suggests they are either unrecognized or ignored. This is supported by a psychiatrist with considerable experience of Mother and Baby Homes who believes that: 'It is too often assumed that an illegitimate pregnancy is simply a bit of bad luck.[2]

ANTE-NATAL CARE AND PREPARATION FOR CONFINEMENT

Routine ante-natal care was carried out in the Home by the general practitioner or the midwife on the staff, at clinics run by the local health authority, or at the hospitals where the girls were to be confined. Sometimes the supervision was undertaken jointly by the clinics or hospitals and the Homes.

Surprisingly, little use was made of relaxation classes. Only three Homes ran classes of their own, and eleven offered no opportunity for expectant mothers to attend classes at all. In the other Homes matrons told us that classes were available at local hospitals or clinics, but it was difficult to discover how widely they were used. Some matrons made classes compulsory and others optional. We were also told that classes sometimes started before the girls came into the Home, and unless a girl had arranged on her own initiative to attend them from the beginning, she could not join later. From the interviews with the residents we formed the opinion that the majority were in favour of classes. Certainly they asked for them in Homes where they were not available. In the Homes where they did attend relaxation classes, how-

[1] Bowlby 1951, Young 1954, Yelloly 1966.
[2] Gough 1964.

ever, neither the pregnant girls nor the mothers were unanimous in their assessment of their value. Some of the negative feelings towards them were almost certainly due to the diffidence the girls felt about attending classes with married women. Although unmarried mothers were addressed as 'Mrs' and rarely treated any differently from any of the other patients, they felt conspicuous, and imagined that the main object of the other patients was to spot the girls without a wedding ring.

As we have seen, the great majority of the residents were having their first baby. Unmarried mothers probably do not want to talk about their pregnancy in the same way as married women and they are likely to be more than ordinarily ignorant and apprehensive about the process of birth. We found it difficult to discover how much instruction they received about this while in the Home. All of the matrons professed themselves willing to talk to the expectant mothers about their confinements. Some occasionally arranged for a midwife or a health visitor to give a talk, but none provided instruction as a matter of routine, and for residents who were unable to get this through ante-natal classes, it seemed that the subject was sometimes not covered at all.

Perhaps the residents were not aware that the matron would give them information for the asking. Group after group wanted someone to tell them what to expect in labour. Many of the expectant mothers were frightened and confused about their approaching confinement. In some cases, so frightened that they preferred to remain ignorant. But these girls were in the minority. The others would have welcomed information. Their urgent wish for knowledge was apparent in their response to the questionnaires. One resident wanted 'talks on easy childbirth'. Another wrote '[we] should be told what to expect when the child is born as some girls do not know and get very frightened when the time is near. There ought to be someone who knows and could help us.' And another, 'she should feel free to ask advice about pregnancy and labour without feeling she was taking up too much of the doctor's time at a clinic. As I am a nurse I feel I should have a good understanding of this, but some girls may not know and are afraid to ask.'

The evidence of the present survey clearly supports the view put forward in the Ministry of Health Survey, that 'preparation for motherhood was not well covered'. In principle, too, it endorses the need for unmarried mothers 'to have the same opportunities for health education as married pregnant women', meaning by this that each group has the same right to adequate care and preparation for childbirth. Whether married and unmarried women should have the same courses, and in particular whether they should attend them together, is a different matter, and one open to question. The problems raised by 'ambiguous maternity' are clearly relevant here. Ordinary anti-natal courses are designed for the married woman. It may be that these are neither a helpful nor a relevant form of preparation for an unmarried mother who may be undecided about her baby's future, planning adoption, or intending to keep her baby in far from normal circumstances. Whether better preparation for childbirth will take the form of special instruction or a greater use of the ordinary services, one further point should be made: if unmarried mothers are to be given the same opportunities as married women, this must include an equal opportunity to decide for themselves whether or not to take advantage of services provided for their benefit.

HOSPITAL CARE

All the mothers from the Before and After Care Homes, and those from the Maternity Homes who had symptoms of a difficult delivery, went to hospital for confinement. None of the matrons reported any difficulty in obtaining hospital beds for their mothers, and most said that the hospitals were co-operative and accepted all cases, even at short notice.

Expectant mothers in labour were sometimes taken to hospital by taxi or in the matron's car. More usually they went by ambulance, and they went alone. In only nine Homes were the mothers always accompanied by a member of the staff. Other matrons either considered it unnecessary to send anyone in the ambulance or were too short staffed to spare anyone. One matron strongly regretted that her young girls had to travel a long way to hospital on their own, but the ambulances used in her area were on radio call and liable to be diverted to any emergency on their return journey from the hospital. Since the matron had been abandoned one night in a remote country village, she had no option but to allow the girls to go unaccompanied. The practice of sending mothers in labour to hospital alone was condemned in the Ministry of Health study and the need to accompany mothers should be borne in mind in staffing the Homes. It would also be an advantage if each Home had a car that could be used for this purpose.

Throughout their stay in hospital the unmarried mothers were always addressed as 'Mrs'. They were usually in an ordinary ward with married patients, though six hospitals put them in a small ward or a single room. The usual period of stay in hospital was about ten days.

One Home took all normal cases back within forty-eight hours of delivery, and three other matrons sometimes had patients discharged to them earlier than usual if the hospital was short of beds.

Usually, the mothers would be visited in hospital by other residents from the Home. Half the matrons allowed visits to hospitals as a matter of course, and six others permitted other residents to visit if the patient had no family or friends going to see her. In most cases this arrangement was made to ensure that a mother would be alone when other visitors came to see her. But one matron felt that, as long as a mother was not entirely neglected during her stay in hospital, there was no need for any visitors from the Home. When two of her residents had been in hospital together, she had not allowed anyone from the Home to go and see them. The mother of one girl had been able to visit and she 'did the necessary' for them both. We did not ask whether the staff visited the mothers in hospital, but five matrons said they tried to do so. Two hospitals were too far away from the Homes for either residents or staff to go during visiting hours. In both these cases committee members and friends of the matrons' tried to see all the mothers who were admitted to them.

In general the matrons considered the standard of medical care good and thought that the unmarried mothers were treated sympathetically by the staff and the other patients. Inevitably there were some criticisms. Two matrons complained that mothers returned from the hospital without breast feeding being properly established, and one added that they had trouble preventing abscesses because the girls had not been properly cared for. One matron was indignant that the hospitals were too busy to teach breast feeding unless a mother really insisted, and another said that she was not always satisfied with the condition of the babies. Of the six matrons who mentioned some dissatisfaction with the hospital care, three were midwives and all made the same complaint: the hospitals were short staffed, overworked, and too busy to give their patients the necessary personal attention. This, said one of them, would be the view of 'any other nurse'.

One matron, when asked whether she was satisfied with the hospital care, replied, 'Oh yes, I am—but some of the girls aren't, though. They want Buckingham Palace you know—the Queen's physician and all that.' This was not evident during our talks with the mothers. On the contrary, their reports of their hospital stay were good. There was warm praise for the nursing staff who often 'spoiled the babies' and 'made a great fuss of them' because they knew they were going to be adopted. The other patients too were usually sympathetic. Some of the mothers made no secret of their single state, and answered a question about their husband with an honest, 'I'm not married'. Others began by making up stories about husbands abroad and at sea, but inevitably the other patients guessed the situation and they usually responded with understanding. One unmarried mother had come back from her hospital stay considerably cheered by the number of other patients in the ward who had 'had to get married'.

Even though most mothers enjoyed their stay, it was not entirely without strain. They were always guarding against being hurt. They found themselves sinking down in bed, trying not to hear the chat about husbands and families, pretending not to mind their difference from the other patients at visiting times. It was then that they felt their loneliness most keenly; the only admiration and congratulations their baby received came from the other girls in the Home. That did not go far to compensate for the pride and delight of the married mother's husband and family.

These were the unavoidable aspects of the hospital stay which made everyone apprehensive. There were some other complaints. A few instances of staff discriminating between married and unmarried patients; of nurses who deliberately tried to embarrass unmarried mothers by talking pointedly of adoption, and enquiring loudly whether a girl was returning to the Mother and Baby Home; and of pressure put on a mother by the nursing staff either to keep or to part with her baby. The matrons told us too that other patients were sometimes cruel. The mothers themselves never mentioned this. What they found hard to bear were thoughtless remarks which were often made with kindly intent. They said it was impossible for other patients to imagine what it was like to have a baby and to face the thought of parting with it. The married patient who had had a third son had no idea how much she wounded an unmarried mother when she said to her, 'I'll have your little girl if you don't want her'. But these people were not unkind—just unimaginative. And they talked of the baby 'as though it were a bag of potatoes or summat'.

THE PLACE OF CONFINEMENT

Opinions were divided as to whether it was preferable for confinement to take place in hospital or in the Mother and Baby Home. Although good reasons were advanced for each point of view, both matrons and residents tended to favour the system they knew.

Current medical policy aims at all deliveries taking place in a well-equipped Maternity Unit. Confinement in a Maternity Home could not approach the safety of a hospital delivery, and this was the point made repeatedly by matrons and residents who favoured a hospital confinement. Two matrons were emphatic that there was a special need for unmarried mothers to be delivered in hospital; almost all are in the group of mothers classified as being 'at risk'[1] during childbirth, because they are having their first baby, and many had had inadequate antenatal care. A third factor, the high neo-natal death rate of illegitimate babies[2] might also argue for the precaution of hospital delivery. Hospital confinement was also seen as a means of keeping the residents in touch with the normal community. They could come to feel very isolated during an unbroken stay of three months in a Mother and Baby Home and even in the Homes where the residents seemed happiest the change occasioned by their visit to hospital was welcomed.

The relative size of Maternity and Before and After Care Homes influenced views on the place of confinement. A Home could only have its own Maternity Unit if it was fairly large, and though the comfort of a Home delivery was admitted by both matrons and girls, many placed a higher value on the relaxed family atmosphere of a small Home. A final practical point raised by matrons was the expense of running Maternity Units and the difficulties of finding qualified midwives.

The main arguments in favour of Maternity Homes, from the residents' point of view, could be summarized in the one word comfort. They shielded them from the painful aspects of hospital they had mentioned. They ensured their privacy, preventing the possibility of a local mother meeting someone she knew in hospital, and they gave them the comfort of delivery by a midwife they knew and trusted. It seemed that in the Maternity Homes the residents developed a deep bond of trust in the staff who would deliver them. As we have seen, many admitted to being 'terrified' and 'absolutely scared stiff' about their confinement, but their growing confidence in their midwives, and the frequent and safe deliveries of other mothers gradually diluted their fear. Nothing was a better antidote to anxiety than the sight of each new mother sitting up in bed drinking a cup of tea, with her baby, only a few minutes old, beside her. The presence of the other girls also helped after the baby's birth, when so many mothers felt very depressed. The matrons considered that the great advantages of Maternity Homes lay in the close continuous relationship between staff

[1] Ministry of Health 1959.
[2] Spicer and Lipworth 1966.

and residents. The value of this relationship and the use made of it have important implications for the purpose of the Homes.

The matrons usually saw the value of continuous care in relation to the delivery itself. They emphasized as the residents had done the benefits of delivery by a known and trusted midwife. Because the mothers had confidence in the staff they relaxed and confinements were easy. We were told that mothers in labour were utterly dependent on their midwife and that a sympathetic midwife could use her patient's trust to comfort her. This was of great value to all the mothers, helping to shape their attitudes to future pregnancies and labours, but it was thought by some to be a special help to the very young girls. The strain of hospital which the older mothers could withstand was too great for the young ones, and three matrons who normally favoured hospital confinements thought that special Maternity Homes should cater for these girls. Three matrons valued the continuous relationship between staff and residents as an effective means of exercising the spiritual aims of the Homes. They saw the mother's vulnerability in the days after confinement as a unique opportunity for spiritual influence. One matron felt that no mother could avoid sensing the presence of the Creator when her baby was born, and this made a tremendous impression on her. Each new mother was asked if she would like to give thanks to God for her baby. Few refused, and for many the prayer in the labour room was the first of their lives. None of the matrons mentioned using the period immediately following the confinement as an opportunity to help the mothers with the problems surrounding their illegitimate maternity. Yet it could be used in this way. Gough has found unmarried mothers particularly responsive to psychotherapy at this time.[1] Because 'all women are particularly in touch with their feelings and problems immediately after childbirth', and because unmarried mothers 'are using illegitimate childbirth as a major way of expressing and dealing with their emotional problems... they are more accessible to help at this time than they have been for years past or are likely to be for many years to come'. He concludes that 'this opportunity is not more widely realized because so few workers have the chance to be with the mothers at this time.'

It would seem, therefore, that there is some conflict between the medical and psychological needs of unmarried mothers during the confinement period. It may be that this cannot entirely be resolved. As a possible means of compromise it was suggested to the matrons that the actual delivery should take place in hospital, and that the

[1] Gough 1964, see also Caplan 1961.

mothers should return to the Mother and Baby Home soon afterwards. With three exceptions this was immediately and firmly rejected; there were neither the staff nor the facilities to provide the care that would be needed. Nevertheless it seemed to us that this pattern of care merits further consideration. It would combine the safety of a hospital delivery with the shelter of the Maternity Home for the greater part of the lying-in period, and with close co-operation between the Home and Hospital it should be possible to establish the mothers' confidence in the Hospital staff.[1] It would relieve the pressure on hospital beds, and in hospitals which normally operate a short period of stay, it would destroy one point of difference between the married and the unmarried patients. Such a change of policy would undoubtedly raise problems of staffing and organization, but these might be overcome with the help of local authority services. It is perhaps significant that the three matrons in favour of this plan had all experienced it in practice.

[1] Chamberlain 1959.

12

THE CARE OF THE BABIES

For mothers planning to keep their baby the post-natal stay in the Mother and Baby Home was a temporary phase, necessary only because they needed time to find somewhere to live or because the rules of the Home required it. For the others, it was their few weeks of practical motherhood before the baby went for adoption and the growing tie between mother and child was cut. For these mothers the problem of short-term or ambiguous maternity is most clearly evident. What is the relationship of a mother to the baby she knows she is giving away? And what part should a mother play in caring for her child while she tries to decide whether or not to keep him? The uniqueness of the situation makes it impossible to draw parallels from other spheres to serve as guides for action. It is a subject of immense importance, and one which urgently requires investigation.

All but two of the Homes visited expected all the mothers to spend a few weeks in the Home caring for their baby. They believed that a girl should fulfil her motherhood and experience the responsibility of looking after her baby. If the mothers kept their child, it was argued, they had a chance to learn to care for him, while those who parted with their baby were comforted to know that for a few weeks at least they had been a 'real' mother. In either case the direct experience of motherhood enabled the residents to appreciate the demands made by a baby on their time and energy, and this helped them towards a realistic decision about the future. This chapter examines the 'mothering situation'—the part played by the mothers in the care of their babies—in the light of these arguments.

When we asked the matrons about the mothers' role in relation to their babies, the answer was always the same, that each mother was entirely responsible for her own baby's care during the whole of her post-natal stay. 'They're their babies,' they said. 'They're their responsibility.' When we went on to enquire in detail about arrangements for the babies' care, it became increasingly obvious that these words meant different things to different people. To one matron it meant that within the necessary safeguards to health, each mother cared for her baby entirely on her own. To another, that the mothers did the baby's washing and were allowed into the nursery to feed him. That was all. Between these two extremes, there was every permutation of freedom and restriction. How and when a baby should be fed, whether a mother could go into the nursery when she liked, or take her baby for a walk, or bath him, were just a few of the issues on which there were different policies.

FEEDING

In only a small number of Homes were the mothers quite free to choose whether to breast feed or bottle feed their babies. In the others they might be encouraged, persuaded, or almost forced, to adopt the method of feeding favoured by those who were looking after them. The pressure could come from the hospitals, the staff at the Home, or both, and it was directed towards bottle feeding as often as breast feeding.

The matrons divided into three equal groups on their feeding policy. One group liked their mothers to breast feed, on the grounds that this fulfilled the maternal cycle, and stimulated the mother-child relationship. Later on, if the baby was adopted, both mother and child would be comforted by the knowledge that the mother had done everything possible for her baby while it was in her care. On a more practical level, breast milk was the 'ideal food' for a baby and it gave rise to less infection than bottle feeding. One matron described breast feeding as 'every baby's birthright'. She was shocked by doctors who asked patients how they would like to feed the baby instead of assuming they would feed him themselves.

The second group of matrons advised their mothers to bottle feed. Amongst them were some who thought that, for babies born within a marriage, breast feeding was the better method, but in the circumstances of an illegitimate birth, the advantages were with bottle feeding. To develop the maternal tie through breast feeding in a mother who would have to part with her baby seemed to them undesirable and even cruel. Forcing an unwilling mother to breast feed was asking for trouble. Some mothers witheld their natural love from a baby they knew they must lose; the baby felt this withdrawal and there could be endless problems. It was also pointed out that almost all the babies would be on to a bottle after the first few weeks anyway. Either they would be adopted, or their mother would be going to work and unable to continue feeding herself. It seemed silly to start breast feeding when it had to be broken off almost as soon as it was established.

The third group of matrons left the mothers to decide for themselves how they would feed. When asked which method they personally preferred, they divided again into advocates of the two methods. Only one matron firmly asserted that babies did equally well either way.

The conflicting views of the matrons reflect the general division of opinion in the medical profession on the relative values of breast feeding. An extensive series of studies into infant feeding carried out at Aberdeen University concluded that there were no grounds for persuading an unwilling mother to breast feed.[1] Since then, however, there has been evidence to suggest that early bottle feeding may be associated with unexplained death in infancy.[2]

The residents' views on the subject of feeding tended to mirror those of the matrons so exactly that it seemed they were merely repeating what they had been told. But in one group, after a few conventional remarks on the values of breast feeding, one girl suddenly and rather shamefacedly confessed that some people were not too keen on it. One after another, the other members of the group supported her, until almost all of them had admitted a revulsion against the idea.

We reached the conclusion that when the residents had their own views on feeding, they were based, like the matrons', on the belief that breast feeding develops the love between a mother and her baby. 'After all,' said one, 'you're giving something of yourself to the baby instead of just sitting there holding a bottle.' Some girls wanted this but most dreaded anything that would deepen the emotional tie with a baby they could not keep. There was also some strong feeling that each mother should be allowed to make her own decision.

If we were uncertain about the views of the majority, we were left in no doubt about the attitudes of a few. Once or twice a nurse in a group would give us all a little lecture on the benefits of breast feeding to both mother and child. Usually, however, the expressions of opinion came from mothers who were opposed to the method of feeding encouraged or imposed in the Home they were in. Thus, some mothers determinedly bottle fed, against advice from hospital nurses, and in spite of accusations of selfishness from the staff of the Homes. And surely the ultimate contradiction was to find two mothers complaining indignantly that they were 'not allowed' to breast feed by a

[1] Hytten *et al.* 1958.
[2] Ministry of Health 1965.

matron who favoured breast feeding, but thought that all the residents wanted to put the babies on the bottle.

Whatever method of feeding was used at birth, most babies would be bottle fed towards the end of their stay in the Home. Usually each mother made up her own baby's feed herself. In one Home the mothers took it in turns under strict supervision from the staff to make up the feeds for all the babies. In five Homes the staff themselves made up the feeds and mothers who were keeping their baby would be taught how to do this before they left. It seems unlikely that this practice would be approved by the Ministry of Health. It was suggested that in several of the Homes visited during the Ministry study that mothers should have had more teaching and practice in the preparation of bottle feeds.

Only one Home had a policy of demand feeding. This was strongly disliked by the mothers. They alleged that they were told to feed their baby not only whenever it cried, but even if it yawned or moved in its cot. They were quite sure that the babies were sometimes overfed and uncomfortable. In the other Homes, the babies were fed according to a time schedule. At least that was the aim, but five matrons said that babies would be fed when they were hungry even if this did not fit into the normal routine. In two Homes the mothers were only allowed three quarters of an hour in which to feed, wind and change their babies and this caused unanimous complaint. 'You can't rush a baby,' the mothers told us. 'You just can't rush a baby, and they make you rush him, and it's no good.'

BATHING

The babies were given their daily bath by their own mother in all but two Homes. In one of these, the staff always bathed the babies, though mothers who were keeping their baby would be taught before they left. In the other Home, the babies were bathed by the staff during the week, and by their mothers on Sundays. The mothers had no chance to get used to handling the baby so the weekly bath was an ordeal. As one explained, 'It's all right when it's got some clothes on, you can grab it, but when it's just in its skin, and it's all slippery, and it's writhing about inside its skin, it's really difficult to hold, and you're just shaking with fright.'

SLEEPING ARRANGEMENTS FOR THE BABIES DURING THE NIGHT

In nine Homes the babies slept in their mothers' bedrooms at night. The rooming-in system was thought by the matrons in these Homes to approximate most closely to the situation in a normal home, and to encourage mothers to be responsible for their own babies. In the other twelve Homes the babies slept in the nursery.[1] The matrons in these Homes preferred this as everyone could sleep undisturbed, and there was no danger of a mother taking her baby into her own bed, falling asleep and suffocating the child. In six Homes night attendants supervized the babies, and in three the mothers took it in turns to sleep in the nursery. In three Homes the babies slept alone. Several matrons warned against the dangers of this and one had good reason to do so; before night attendants were employed in her Home, three babies had died.

NURSERY RULES

In just under half of the Homes, the mothers were free to go into the nursery and see their babies whenever they wished, though they would usually be discouraged from 'haphazard' or 'indiscriminate picking up'. Some matrons liked the mothers to look in on their babies frequently, and one complained that they did not go into the nursery often enough, 'they'd rather have a smoke'. In the other Homes, the mothers were only supposed to go into the nursery at feeding times. Two or three matrons expected the girls to attend to crying babies in between times but six enforced the nursery rules strictly, and a mother could only go to her baby if she asked permission or if she was sent for by one of the staff. One matron explained that this ruling was necessary because some girls, including expectant mothers, were such a nuisance; always running in to pick up and cuddle the babies. The other matrons gave no explanations.

In all the Homes, the babies were put outside in prams to sleep whenever the weather permitted. Usually, mothers were allowed to take the babies out in their prams during their free time in the afternoons, but seven matrons would not allow this. Two enforced a ban on pram pushing after they had discovered that the mothers were taking the babies into local parks, and admiring strangers were giving them lollipops and lumps of chocolate. The other five matrons offered no reason for keeping the babies in the grounds.

The Homes, and sometimes different members of staff in the same Home, varied greatly in the contact they permitted between residents'

[1] In one Home we had no information on this point and the Home for schoolgirls had no accommodation for babies. If the mother returned to the Home after the birth of her baby, the child was fostered until an adoption placement could be made or until the mother left the Home.

visitors and their babies. Only a few let the mothers take their babies with them when they went out with visitors. When this was not permitted, there were many complaints that visitors were allowed only the briefest glimpses of the baby. Contact with the baby was limited as a precaution against infection, but some of the mothers thought that grandparents should be able to cuddle their grandchild, if only for a moment, and in one Home the residents were particularly indignant that the matron's dog could wander into the nursery at will while their parents had to be content with a peep through the window.

As well as these general rules, individual Homes had their own traditions in the nursery. Two matrons allowed the mothers to go out for a day provided that they asked someone else to take care of the baby. This was a popular arrangement; the mothers enjoyed their freedom and the expectant mothers became accustomed to handling a baby. Other customs were not so popular. The residents in one Home thought it was stupid to put the baby on the pot after each feed. In another Home they could not understand why the matron went round twice each day waking the babies to be washed and changed a full hour or half hour before they were due to be fed, so that they were left screaming until feed time. And in another, the babies had to be dressed in shabby clothes belonging to the Home, although the mothers would have much preferred to use the clothes that they had provided for them.

REVIEW OF THE 'MOTHERING SITUATION'

At first, the girls, like any new mother, needed advice and instruction on caring for their baby. All the Homes gave them some teaching, though its quality varied. Thirteen Homes had qualified midwives or trained children's or nursery nurses to advise in the nursery. One matron had neither training nor experience of baby care, and she said she managed with the baby in one hand and a copy of 'Dr Spock' in the other. After the initial teaching the mother took charge herself in about half the Homes, though help was always at hand if it was needed. In the other Homes, the staff continued to supervise the mothers closely. This was a source of irritation. The mothers wanted their babies to themselves, and resented a constant stream of instructions, particularly when different members of staff told them to do things in different ways. They complained that some of the staff were not as careful as they should be when they handled the baby. Yet there would be 'terrible trouble if you do something wrong'. The mothers were willing to accept advice but some of them found this public criticism of their handling of their babies upsetting, and 'After all, it's your baby'.

To the mothers it rarely seemed that they were fulfilling their motherhood. In this respect they felt disappointed. It did not seem to them that they were responsible for their babies, though they wanted to be and they had expected to be. Instead, some of them felt that they were little more than nurse maids, feeding the baby and doing its washing. The most common cause of disappointment was the lack of opportunity to cuddle and play with the baby; 'In fact,' we were told in one Home, 'there's no mothering allowed at all.' Some girls accepted the matrons' explanations that contact with the baby was restricted to prevent mothers from growing too attached to a baby who was going to be adopted, and acknowledged that this was for the best. There were not many who took this view. It was far more common to feel that 'you don't have your baby for very long, and you want as much of it as you can during that period'.

Obviously, from a practical point of view a mother in a Mother and Baby Home cannot have sole charge of her baby exactly as she would at home. When a group of mothers and babies are living together, standards of health and hygiene must be maintained and some supervision is necessary. Equally staff must ensure that babies are not neglected by mothers who are physcially and mentally incapable of looking after a child. Even so, in many Homes the supervision and restrictions on the care of the baby went far beyond what was necessary. It may be difficult for trained and competent staff to stand by and watch an inexperienced mother's clumsy handling of her baby but it should be recognized that most of the mothers are quite capable of caring for their babies; many are of an age when they might be married and bringing up their legitimate children. Staff were too ready to take to themselves responsibilities which properly belonged to the mothers, and which in all but a few cases could safely be left to them. An extreme example of this was of a baby who was operated on without his mother's knowledge. Following the operation it was some time before the mother discovered that the hospital staff were ringing up daily to report on the child's progress; they spoke to the matron not to the baby's mother.

It seems urgently necessary for Homes to re-examine their practice in the nursery and the objects of the post-natal stay. These cannot be reconciled at the moment. If the aim of the Home is to enable a girl to be a mother to her child, if she is to develop a sense of responsibility towards the baby, and if the post-natal stay is to help her make a realistic decision about the future, then the unmarried mother must have the same responsibility for her child as a married mother. She must be free to go to her child when she wishes, to show her baby to her family, and to dress the child in the clothes she has brought for him. These are simple and basic responsibilities. They are also the rights of a mother. If unmarried mothers are denied these rights, the Homes must ask themselves what they are doing. Why do they restrict the mother's role? What benefit is there to the baby in a contact with his mother that is limited to feeding and occasional bath times? Can he get anything from such a relationship that he would not get in a good nursery? What effect does restricted motherhood have on the mothers? What *is* the purpose of the post-natal stay?

13

RELIGION IN THE HOMES

Because of the concern so often expressed over the religious setting of residential care for unmarried mothers, it was a special point of this study to enquire into the religious practices in the Homes, and the residents' reactions towards them. This issue was of little relevance to the four local health authority Homes. Their concern was for the practical and social needs of the unmarried mothers, and they offered no organized religious activity or teaching. These Homes had no chapels and no chaplains, though the residents were free to go to church if they wished. In the voluntary homes the situation was different; all those visited were church Homes, run by church people, assisted from church funds and staffed by church workers. In contrast to the local health authorities 'the end of the work done in the name of the Church is not merely material assistance or even social rehabilitation, although these may be assumed to be part of it, it is spiritual redemption.[1] The Christian faith was the cornerstone of the Homes. This was repeatedly apparent in the attitudes of the staff to their work and in the extent to which religion and religious practices featured in the day to day life of the Homes.

RELIGIOUS ACTIVITIES IN THE VOLUNTARY HOMES

The matron held daily prayers in all but two of the Homes. The services were usually short and simple; a hymn, some prayers, a Bible reading, and perhaps a short address. Three Homes held prayers twice a day, and at one Home each of the services lasted for half an hour. Communion Services were usually held weekly or monthly, but two matrons preferred to arrange these only when a number of communicants in the Home wished it.

Generally, the residents were expected to go to church on Sundays. In some Homes only the pregnant girls had to go; in other Homes,

[1] Hall and Howes 1965.

the mothers went, though some matrons excused anyone within a certain period of their confinement. Two Homes provided alternatives of a recorded service or private prayer in the chapel for those who stayed behind. Usually, everyone, of whatever denomination, went to the same church, but one matron allowed residents to choose their own church. Two other matrons thought it wrong to insist on church attendance, and made no arrangements for their residents to go. In one of these Homes, the residents were free to go to church if they wished; few did. In the other, the residents told us that they were 'not allowed to go to church'. They seemed to be upset by this, and one girl had told the matron she would like to go to church, and the matron had agreed to take her one Sunday.

There were other services, too, for special occasions. All the babies in the Roman Catholic Homes were baptized, and those in the Salvation Army Homes were dedicated. In the other Homes babies were sometimes christened or a service of blessing held for those who were to be adopted. Occasionally, we were told one of the residents themselves asked to be baptized. At one Home, all the mothers were churched when they returned from hospital. From time to time, too, there were marriages from the Homes. In all the Homes grace was said at mealtimes.

Attendance at Services
In six Homes participation in the religious life of the Home was a condition of entry, set out on the application forms. It seemed likely however that other Homes relied on social workers to inform their clients of similar rulings, and in one of these a resident who refused to attend daily prayers was asked to leave. Several matrons told us that there were no formal requirements, it was simply hoped that everyone would attend church and chapel. No one would be forced to go against her will. All the same, everybody went. We did not find one resident who stayed away from the daily services in the chapel. Nor were there any Homes in which they realized they were free to do so. It was the same with church-going. Only in one Home did both matron and residents agree that they went to church or not as they chose. One matron told us that it was stupid and old-fashioned to send people to church against their will. Yet the residents in her home maintained they *had* to go; everyone was 'shoved' into the car whether they wanted to go to church or not. Even if they had a choice (which they doubted) nobody would dare refuse; there would be such a fuss.

In spite of the pressure the residents felt to attend church and chapel, they raised few objections. There were complaints from one Home where everyone went to the same high Anglican Church, and the girls were under the impression that they were attending a 'Catholic Mass'. They could not understand what was going on; the incense made them feel sick, and they wished they could have a service of their own in the Home. There was also a small number of girls who thought they should be allowed to go to their own churches. Otherwise, though there was little enthusiasm for church, most people were content to go if it pleased the matron.

The services in the Home were accepted in much the same spirit. Indeed the residents seemed to enjoy the daily services. It was a break in the day; they had a good sing. They were even surprised when we asked if they had any objections. Why should they? And 'after all', was the attitude, 'this is a church Home and it's only ten minutes a day anyway'. There were some complaints. There was a little opposition to compulsory Communion Services. Many of the expectant mothers found it tiring and uncomfortable to kneel for so long, and there was a general feeling that non-communicants should not be obliged to attend. There were objections too from the Home which had two half-hour services each day; that was too much. Another complaint came from a group who said that no one minds prayers, but 'they do tend to push your sins at you—not in so many words, but the implication is there'. And in another Home, after five members of the group had declared no objection to attending chapel, the sixth girl thought for a bit, and then said, 'Well, I don't know, I think religion is pushed at you in this place.' The others looked at her in surprise, but there were laughs and agreement all round when she continued, 'Well, you wouldn't go to chapel every morning after breakfast normally, would you?' The weekly visits to church and the daily services in the chapel were certainly not a feature of normal everyday life. Only a quarter of the residents had been to church once a month or more during the year before they came into the Home. Half had never been at all.

Chaplains
All of the Church of England Homes and the two Roman Catholic Homes had their own chaplains. The Free Church Home had the services of a number of Nonconformist Ministers, and the Methodist Deaconess and the Salvation Army Officers did their own ministering. Church of England chaplains usually went to the Homes regularly to take the weekly or monthly communion service. Sometimes they also took other short services during the week. Six held weekly talks

and discussion groups with the girls. These were not necessarily confined to religious topics; social and moral issues might also be discussed. Two chaplains whom we saw, and several matrons, stressed the importance of talking to the residents 'on their own level' and 'in terms they can understand'. It was essential to capture their interest, and several of the chaplains were said to have a gift for this.

Most chaplains would also see the residents individually two or three times during their stay. At one Home, where this service was not available because the chaplain was ill, the residents missed it. They felt that many people found it easier to confide in a chaplain than in anybody else. In our discussion we concentrated on the chaplains' ministrations to the residents, but one chaplain pointed out that the staff also came under his care. He saw the task of 'ministering to those who minister' as an important part of his work, and believed that chaplains could do much to support staff in this way.

Referrals to the Parish Priest

After leaving the Home, the residents could be referred to the care of their parish priest. This was seen as a way of drawing a girl into the Christian community of her home town, and in six Homes the matrons and chaplains were very anxious that it should be done. They would rarely, however, make a referral without the resident's consent, though in one Roman Catholic Home all residents were automatically referred to their local priest unless there was a strong reason against it. Two Anglican Homes had at one time made similar automatic referrals, though both had discontinued the practice. One of the matrons stopped when she discovered that some of the clergy had been going round to unmarried mothers and saying, 'I hear you had an illegitimate baby in . . .'. Since then, she had been much more careful, and only referred to ministers whom she knew would handle the situation tactfully. The other matron, and the chaplain, would still have liked to refer every resident, but they told us, 'We got such a roasting from some of the moral welfare workers over this confidentiality business that we gave it up'.

Religious Instruction

Apart from the discussion groups held by the chaplains, there was little formal religious education in the Homes. One Roman Catholic Home ran a course of instruction for those who were said to have lapsed from the faith, or whose allegiance to Roman Catholicism was only nominal. Two matrons used the daily service to explain passages from the Bible, one to give a talk appropriate to one or more of the residents, and some held occasional group meetings. Others simply waited for an opportunity; 'all the usual questions about life, living and suffering' would be discussed as they arose. Confirmation classes could be arranged if necessary in most Homes, but matrons preferred to test a resident's enthusiasm and let her wait for confirmation until she reached home. A certain amount of preparation could be done by the chaplain if a resident really wanted this.

VIEWS ON SPIRITUAL CARE

Matrons' Views
Concern for the spiritual well-being of the residents was part of every matron's work, though the relative emphasis laid on this and other aspects of the job was an individual matter. Some matrons saw their main task as giving practical help to people in difficulties. The hope that the residents would derive spiritual benefit from living in a Christian Home appeared almost incidental, and one matron admitted to doing little on the spiritual side. Others put this first. They described themselves as 'pastoral' and 'missionary' workers. Their vocation was to inspire others to share their faith, and it was this rather than the practical problems of illegitimate maternity that drew them to moral welfare work.

There was a widespread belief among the matrons that to force religion on the residents was futile. One matron told us that she had once worked as an assistant in a church Home where there was 'a solid hour of prayers every morning'. She knew how the girls reacted against this. It militated against the effect it was trying to achieve, and she herself held no daily prayers in her own Home. Preaching was held to be less effective than example, and the most potent force of all was the influence of a Christian community of staff working together. Some of the Homes did place great emphasis on organized worship, and these were the matrons who took most trouble to convince us that 'We are not forever ramming it [religion] down their throats'. As one explained, the residents are 'taken into prayers and faced with the truth'. Then it is up to them to respond if they wish. But if a resident comes and says, 'Matron, why is it that you are so happy? Why don't I feel happy like you?' then the staff can step in with their spiritual work. We were continually told of the need for a sensitive handling of religion; 'a careful and prayerful approach' was how one matron described it.

About one third of the matrons thought that the residents responded well to religion while they were in the Home. They said that the girls were strengthened and found their consciences eased by the practice of their religion. One thought that after a time in the Home they mellowed and became more responsive. Another saw the period of pregnancy as a gradual breaking down of a girl's hostility and resistance to religion; the Lord made His presence felt in the Home and, after a time, residents were able to come to Him without embarrassment. The remaining two thirds of the matrons did not see such a positive response. They described the residents as 'apathetic'. Few ever voiced any objections to the services they were asked to attend. Some even got 'quite a taste for going to church', but even amongst those who had been regular churchgoers there appeared to be little 'real religious faith or experience'. It was something that had been left out of their lives altogether.

Although most matrons saw no dramatic spiritual gains amongst the girls during their stay, they hoped and believed that the atmosphere of the Christian community did have some effect. They were satisfied if the residents began to think about things, and several matrons thought that their work might come to fruition after a girl had left. They told us of letters received from past residents telling them that they were now going to church or asking for their prayers when they were in difficulties. Social workers on the other hand considered that the Christian message made a lasting impact on only a tiny fraction of the residents. As far as her 'ordinary little girls' were concerned, said one worker, it was 'like water off a duck's back'.

Residents' Views

The residents themselves gave very little indication of any positive appreciation of the spiritual care they received, or of any hostility towards it. The great majority simply accepted the unaccustomed practice of religion as 'part of the artificial situation in which their unwanted maternity had landed them'.[1] In three or four Homes however there was some feeling, in spite of the matrons' assurances to the contrary, that religion was 'pushed' on to them. This was so, particularly in one Home where we were told that 'their main aim in this Home is to convert you'. But the complaints were few. They were delivered mildly, and they were almost equally balanced by favourable comments. Strong views in either direction were rare. The girl who declared that

[1] Hall and Howes 1965. A similar passive acceptance of religious activities was noted in the Ministry of Health study.

she did not need God, that she could get on perfectly well without Him, and that she wished they would shut up about Him, was as exceptional as one who saw the greatest value of the Home in the fact that she would attend church regularly after she left. Evidence of real spiritual involvement in the religious life of the Homes was almost negligible. Equally, there was little to suggest that participation in the religious activities offended many consciences. The overwhelming mood was one of amiable, tolerant apathy.

REVIEW OF THE RELIGIOUS PURPOSE OF VOLUNTARY HOMES

All this perhaps suggests that the religious purposes of Mother and Baby Homes were irrelevant, and achieved nothing. Yet this was not entirely true. The religious associations of the voluntary Homes could be seen to have positive results. This was evident in the feeling expressed, and very much appreciated by the residents that staff showed a genuine personal concern for them as individuals. Our impression, though it would be hard to substantiate, was that this feeling of personal concern arose out of the staff's interest in the spiritual well-being of the residents. Even when the girls were quite indifferent to the religious approach as such, they seemed to value interest shown in themselves for some reason other than the immediate problems of their pregnancy. Perhaps also they gained some sense of individual worth from the staff's regard for them as potential members of the Church.

In turn, the fact that the staff in the voluntary Homes had specifically chosen to work for the Church seemed to influence the residents, regard for them. Again, even when religion had no meaning for the residents, they acknowledged its worth and respected its importance for the staff. Quite often they interpreted particular examples of kindness on the part of a member of staff as associated with their religious beliefs.

Finally, though this was not a specific subject of enquiry, it seemed likely that the religious affiliations of the voluntary Homes had considerable importance for the staff. Hall and Howes noted the significance for moral welfare workers of working as 'part of a company commissioned by the church'. And as we have seen it was caring for the spiritual needs and not the medical, social or emotional problems of unmarried mothers that some staff regarded as their real work. Because of this, it might be supposed that the relative emphasis on religion in the Homes would affect the recruitment and retention of staff. There is however only weak evidence from the present survey to support such a theory.

The religious associations of voluntary Homes must also be examined in a wider context. Their spiritual aims have long been a focus of public indignation. To many, it seems wrong that as a condition of receiving practical or social work help, an unmarried mother must accept, or at least acquiesce in beliefs and practices which may be irrelevant or even repugnant to her.[1] There was no suggestion, however, in spite of the strong religious emphasis in some Homes, that any resident felt compelled to make a hypocritical declaration of belief in a faith she did not share. At the same time it was inevitable that in all the church Homes there was some pressure towards conformity with religious practices, even where none was intended.

The church Homes and social workers countered criticisms of their religious aims with a reminder that the residents enter the Homes voluntarily. Social workers usually tell their clients about the religious practices, and anyone to whom these are unacceptable can decline the offer of a place. In this sense an unmarried mother does choose whether or not she will go into a church Home. Few, however, can have a realistic choice. As we have seen, out of 172 known Mother and Baby Homes, only thirty-four are provided by bodies which do not form part of a church organization. Unmarried mothers who really need accommodation may have to go into a church Home, however unwillingly, simply because other sections of the community do so little for them. This is the fact that should be the real target for public criticism.

Though there may be difficulties in combining religious aims with other aspects of care, the right of church Homes to pursue a spiritual purpose must be acknowledged. Some of the Homes visited exhibited an uncertainty of the relative emphasis that should be given to their different objectives and this is something that needs to be determined. Yet, however the Homes define and carry out their different purposes, the religious setting of residential care for unmarried mothers must continue as long as the community is content to leave the provision of Mother and Baby Homes to the churches. If this is unacceptable, then the energy now expended on criticizing the church Homes would be more appropriately directed towards providing a secular alternative.

---

[1] P. E. P. 1946.

14

SOCIAL WORK IN THE HOMES

In this chapter, dealing with arrangements for social work in the Homes, we touch on another of the services for unmarried mothers. The general provision of social work services, including after-care and the help given by a social worker during the early months of pregnancy, were outside our terms of reference; casework help has only been considered in so far as it is a necessary part of the care provided in a Mother and Baby Home.

ARRANGEMENTS FOR SOCIAL WORK IN THE HOMES

Arrangements for social work while the residents were in the Homes varied from Home to Home and from social worker to social worker. Perhaps the general lack of agreement amongst matrons and social workers, as to who should have the major responsibility for social work in the Mother and Baby Home can be traced to the development of moral welfare work and to the fact that 'outdoor work' grew out of the earlier residential care.

The great majority of social workers and just over half the matrons took the view that the social worker should continue to hold the major responsibility for casework while the client was in the Home. Surprisingly, they laid little stress on the importance of a continuous relationship, or on the work that could be done by an outdoor worker with the residents' families. Instead, they argued that the matrons were not trained in casework techniques,[1] that matrons were 'too much on top of the girls' to act in a casework capacity, and that the residents needed to turn to someone outside the Home if they were unhappy there. Four matrons considered they should have the sole responsibility for casework, and about one-fifth of the social workers agreed with them (though half of them complained that the matrons did not fulfil this duty adequately). Those who took this view held that as the

[1] 8 of the 23 matrons in our sample were trained moral welfare workers.

matrons lived with the residents they became better acquainted with them than an outdoor worker and as they were always on hand, they were better placed to help. In addition to these two main groups, one matron said she 'shared' the casework with the outdoor workers, and five said they might or might not take over the social work, depending on which social worker had been dealing with the case before admission.

With all these different opinions it was not at all clear what would happen to a client if both the matron and the social worker were expecting to hold the major responsibility for casework, or if each considered that this role belonged to the other. Nor was it surprising that we received complaints from both groups. The matrons thought that outdoor workers did not show enough interest in their clients; they did not know them well, they were never there when a crisis arose and they simply did not give the residents the support they needed. The social workers complained that the matrons lacked the competence to undertake casework, and that they interfered. One matron was said to make residents who were planning adoption feel so guilty that some mothers altered their decision even though their plans for keeping the baby were quite unrealistic. It was unusual for either matron or social worker to relinquish completely all claims to provide some degree of support, and those who had worked together over a period of time generally evolved a pattern of responsibility which suited them both.

CONTACT BETWEEN SOCIAL WORKERS AND RESIDENTS

All but eight of the girls who completed a questionnaire were in touch with a social worker and Table 10 shows the kinds of social workers helping them.

The great majority of social workers continued to see their clients while they were in the Homes. We were told that the usual arrangement was to visit 'once or twice' before the baby was born to see that a girl was 'settling down' and that 'she had no problems', and 'once or twice' afterwards to discuss plans and make arrangements for the baby's future. The number of visits might be increased or decreased according to the needs of the client and the worker's judgement of the matron's ability to provide necessary support. Workers whose office was near a Home saw their clients more frequently than those who had to travel some distance to the Homes they used; all the Homes used by one moral welfare worker were too far away to visit, and she said that letters had to take the place of interviews. There was a little variation in the

Table 10

Kinds of Social Workers helping Residents during stay in Homes

Social Workers	NORTH Number of girls	%	SOUTH Number of girls	%	TOTAL Number of girls	%
Church of England Moral Welfare	94	64.8	47	49.4	141	58.7
Roman Catholic Moral Welfare	5	3.4	20	21.1	25	10.4
Child Care	11	7.6	13	13.7	24	10.0
Local Health Authority	12	8.3	—	0.0	12	5.0
Probation	2	1.4	5	5.3	7	2.9
Medical Social Worker	3	2.1	2	2.1	5	2.1
Other	3	2.1	—	0.0	3	1.3
No Social Worker	6	4.1	2	2.1	8	3.3
No Information	9	6.2	6	6.3	15	6.3
TOTALS	145	100	95	100	240	100

amount of visiting undertaken by the different types of workers. Child care officers, and local health authority welfare workers visited more often than most moral welfare workers, though two local health authority officers considered their responsibility ceased on a client's admission to a Mother and Baby Home, and did not visit at all.

Few of the moral welfare workers were satisfied with the care they were able to offer their clients in the Homes. They saw them too infrequently; caseloads were too heavy, lack of secretarial help meant that much time was spent on administration, and travelling consumed a large part of their working hours. One worker summed up the general feeling of frustration and dissatisfaction by saying that understaffing was so acute it was inevitable that they should be grossly inefficient in many ways. They had no time to build up good relationships with their clients over a number of interviews, and it was almost impossible to apply the term casework to the relationship they established.

RELATIONSHIP BETWEEN RESIDENTS AND SOCIAL WORKERS

The truth of this assessment became evident during the group discussions on social work. The value of casework was demonstrated forcefully by a small proportion of residents (about 15 per cent) who did seem to have a good relationship with their social workers. These residents spoke with genuine appreciation of the help they received. They often described at length and in detail how understanding the social worker had been, how helpful in supplying practical information about the Homes or grants or adoption arrangements, and how they 'could talk anything out with her'. The use these residents had apparently made of their relationship with their social workers, and the warmth with which they spoke of them, made a sharp contrast to the vagueness and indifference exhibited by the majority of residents.

Nice, kind people who would help you if they could; that was the typical verdict on the social workers. Residents had little understanding of their role. In one Home the sole function ascribed to social workers was to recover the baby if mothers who had decided on adoption changed their minds. A few residents knew that social workers could help in obtaining grants, and finding jobs, or a foster home for the baby. To the great majority, however, the social worker was someone who arranged for them to come into the Home, and who sometimes helped with the adoption. That, as far as they could see, was all. 'You seem to lose touch with them once you come into the Home,' one resident explained. This was borne out by our data on the social workers visits to the Homes. One hundred and five girls, nearly half of those in touch with a social worker, had not been visited by a social worker since they came into the Home. 36 per cent of these residents had been in the Home less than 2 weeks, but 30 per cent had been there for more than 6 weeks. Of the residents who had seen their social worker, the great majority had had only one or two interviews. Less than 30 had seen a social worker 3 times or more. Many of the residents had been told to contact their workers if they needed help, but they knew they were busy, and did not like to bother them for 'just a little worry'. Clearly the residents did not see their social worker as the person to whom they would naturally turn to discuss any plans or difficulties. Some took their troubles to the matron. Others simply looked to the other residents for comfort and support.

NEED FOR SOCIAL WORK HELP

Casework with unmarried mothers in a Mother and Baby Home could have two objectives; to support and assist a resident in making plans for her baby, and to help her to resolve the more basic problems of adjustment of which the illegitimate pregnancy may be a symptom. Neither of these objectives seemed to be achieved.

All the residents we saw were within weeks of deciding whether to keep or to part with their baby. Yet they had only the haziest notions of what either solution would mean in practical or emotional terms. In all but a few cases they were ignorant of the most basic facts about adoption or the facilities they might find helpful if they kept the baby. They relied largely on each other for information, and this probably accounted for many of the misconceptions they held. There was, for instance, a common belief that if a mother wanted to have her baby adopted she would have to look after the child herself for several months, unless she came into a Mother and Baby Home. In one Home the residents had recently seen a television programme about adoption and gathered that some disapproval attached to 'third parties'. They were mystified as to who or what these were, but not too worried because, one of them remarked, 'there don't seem to be any third parties here'.

There was similar doubt and uncertainty on many topics. Simple matters of fact such as whether or not a resident would receive a bill at the end of her stay caused worries which should have been easy to remove. There were complaints that residents asked for information from their social workers but never received a straight answer. Different girls were told different things. This caused considerable anxiety; no one knew what to believe. At least part of this confusion could probably be explained by the fact that the residents in the Homes came from so many different areas. Different adoption societies have different rules and procedures, and different local authorities make different rulings on financial matters. If this was the explanation, it was not understood by the residents.

With so much evidence of ignorance and confusion, it is difficult to avoid the impression that social workers do not take the time and trouble to ensure that their clients understand the situation within the limits of their capacity. A contributory factor to the confusion may be found in the tense and worried condition of the residents. In this state of mind, detailed factual matters are not easily absorbed, and social workers may have to repeat information and explanations several times before they are fully understood. To overcome these difficulties, it might be helpful to arrange group talks and discussions on topics such as fostering or adoption procedure. Simple leaflets explaining the available services would also help to avoid mistaken ideas and confusion.

Factual matters, financial worries, finding jobs, or somewhere to live were all problems that arose in discussions. None of them had any real significance beside the decision about the baby. The residents came back to this time and again. It was forever on their minds. They were desperate to sort things out, but they had no-one to talk to except someone else who was just as worried. The social workers were not there, and most of the matrons would not discuss plans for the baby until the child was two or three weeks old. Any discussion before then was a waste of time, the matrons told us, because so many of the residents changed their minds later. Some matrons did send for the mothers when the baby was two or three weeks old. Others waited until a mother came to them. Only then would they discuss the plans she had made, and attempt to assess whether her decision to keep or to part with the child was a final one.

Most of the expectant mothers were planning adoption. They were unsettled by repeated assertions from matrons and social workers that they would change their minds when the baby was born. Yet they acknowledged the truth of these warnings. Some of the mothers did change their minds, and others 'nearly go demented' making wild plans for trying to keep the child although they know it is really impossible. This change of mind was evident in the answers to our questionnaire. The percentage of mothers planning to keep their babies (22.5 per cent) was almost double that of the pregnant girls (13.2 per cent).[1] Whether or not the answers given represented the plans that would finally be implemented we had no means of knowing. Gough stresses that 'once the baby is born the mother nearly always (at least temporarily) reverses any previous decision to part with her baby,'[2] and it may be that some of the answers we were given resulted from such temporary reversals of plan.

Recent writings and research on the subject suggests that the final outcome of the mother's decision will become apparent during the ante-natal period, and Meyer et al,[3] using background characteristics known to the agency helping the unmarried mothers, made a correct prediction of the final decision for about 80 per cent of the cases. Though this appears to be the only attempt at prediction, it is widely held that the factors which can be expected to determine the mother's decision can be identified before the birth of the baby, and that with the aid of a good social worker, many mothers can be helped towards a realistic assessment of the situation during their pregnancy.[4] Though the final decision or a reassessment of plans made in the ante-natal

---

[1] This difference was significant at the 0·1 per cent level.
[2] Gough 1964.
[3] Meyer et al 1966.
[4] Bowlby 1951; Thompson 1956; Yelloly 1965; Young 1954; Gough 1964; Ball 1962.

period may have to await the baby's birth, it would appear that any dramatic reversal of a previous decision is likely to occur within a short time of the delivery. All this would argue the need for discussion of the girl's plans during pregnancy and soon after delivery—the very times when such discussion is least likely to be offered.

Great stress is laid by the same authorities on the need for plans made during the ante-natal period to be flexible. Gough warns that 'the too ready acceptance of a pregnant girl's decision about the future of her baby is a great disservice to the girl and will deep down be very much resented'. In our view the pregnant girl should be assured that any plans made in the ante-natal period are only tentative and that they can be revised. It may also be wise to warn her that she may feel differently after her baby is born. Equally, however, too much insistence on her expected change of mind may not be helpful. A dismissal of her intended plans during pregnancy as irrelevant will certainly be a disservice. The matrons and the social workers should be ready to discuss the problem of a girl's decision whenever and as often as she wishes.

There can be no more difficult decision than the one an unmarried mother has to make about her baby. Ball urges social workers 'to accept a personal involvement in the situation', arguing that girls 'welcome the interest of an outsider with whom to discuss their problems' particularly when they are unable to do this with their own families, and that many of the girls 'who continue to vacilate are indirectly requesting help with a decision they do not want to make alone'. Yet the matrons emphasized that a mother should be left to make the decision on her own. One matron expressed the general feeling by saying that she would never dare have it on her conscience that she had encouraged a girl to either solution. We were also told of attempts to discourage parents from influencing their daughters decision, and the efforts of one matron in this direction have already been described. The residents themselves realized the need for the final decision to be their own. At the same time they needed to talk about it. They talked and talked to each other (and as we described, they even talked to us when they had the chance). That helped them a little, but what they really needed was someone who could help them to grasp the problem. They did not want anyone else to make their decision for them; they stressed that repeatedly. They did want information: someone who could tell them all the factors they should consider, and who could help them to foresee the consequences of their decision. And they wanted to talk it over again and again.

Primarily, the girls wanted help in coming to their decision. Then they wanted to know the practical and emotional meaning of their decision, in particular of the decision to surrender their baby for adoption. There was little evidence to suggest that much was done to help in this direction. Some matrons mentioned that the residents' families did not understand the need to allow a mother to grieve over parting with the baby, but it seemed that matrons themselves did not always appreciate this. In one Home, the residents described how the difficulty of handing over the baby for adoption was made worse by the knowledge that the matron was standing watching. If they showed any sign of being upset, she would say, 'Well, it's your own fault. If you're upset about the baby you shouldn't have given it away.'

If the residents were given little support in the emotional problems directly arising from their pregnancy, there was nothing to suggest that the more basic problems of adjustment received any attention. In this respect it would seem that the Homes have changed little since the survey taken by the Ministry of Health. Their views accord with ours, that although practical problems were dealt with helpfully and kindly, casework support in emotional and social difficulties was not generally available; indeed it is doubtful how far this was even recognized as necessary. It appears that the lack of a casework relationship is not limited to the unmarried mothers who go into Mother and Baby Homes. In a study group formed by representatives of hospitals and social service agencies assisting unmarried mothers in Cardiff it was agreed that 'too often, the unmarried mothers seemed to be offered courses of action rather than a relationship, and she might be seen by a series of social workers and yet not get real help from any of them'.[1] Although a study of 135 cases assisted by the agencies listed only sixteen in which no social or psychological problems were found, the unmarried mothers were rarely offered a relationship in terms of 'someone who cared and who would be available for talking to, for giving help, to speak to about problems and their meaning and ways of working them out'. Social casework with unmarried mothers is all the more urgently needed if it is considered that illegitimate pregnancy is rarely accidental and is in fact a desperate way of seeking help with problems of which the mother herself is only dimly conscious.[2] It is sometimes said that unless the underlying tensions and conflicts motivating an illegitimate pregnancy are resolved a girl may continue to repeat the pregnancy in successive attempts to work out her diffi-

[1] Jacobs 1964.
[2] Gough 1961.

culties.[1] To some extent matrons and social workers acknowledge the dangers of a subsequent illegitimate pregnancy if an unmarried mother received inadequate help. It appeared, however, that this was always seen as following a 'wrong' decision for a baby to be adopted; the second child being known as the 'replacement baby'. The situation was never described to us in terms of a deeper conflict.

MEETING THE NEED FOR CASEWORK

In considering how the need for casework might be met four factors should be mentioned. The first—the shortage of staff and the need for matrons to be freed from housekeeping and administrative duties to turn their attentions to the residents has already been discussed.

The second factor is the lack of agreement on the respective roles of matrons and social workers. It seemed to us that both should share in supporting the residents during their stay in the Home. In individual cases the respective roles of matron and social worker may be partly determined by the quality of relationship each makes with the client. In general, however, it should be possible to distinguish their separate functions. The 'outdoor' worker is the one most appropriately placed to hold a continuous relationship with the girl; she will have been supporting her through the early months of pregnancy; and it is she who has the best opportunity to work with the clients' family and the baby's father, and to help the girl herself after she leaves the Mother and Baby Home. The outdoor worker, too, may generally be regarded as the specialist in arranging adoption or the use of other services which the unmarried mother may need. The chief role of the matron, on the other hand, is to create what the Williams Committee described as a 'harmonious group' and to provide for the residents the environment in which they can best be helped to work through their difficulties. Because the matrons live with the residents they can form a more personal relationship with them than the social worker; for some girls the matron will be a mother figure; for others her role will be that of a sympathetic sensible friend. However their specific roles are defined, the matron and the social worker must work together. It is essential that there should be the fullest co-operation between them and every effort should be made to ensure that each understands and respects the work of the other.

Thirdly, there is the fact that whenever matrons or social workers

[1] See for example proceedings of a Conference 'Pregnancy in Adolescence' N.C.U.M.C. 1966.

spoke of helping the residents with their problems they always referred to support given on the basis of individual interviews. There was never any suggestion that the group of residents could itself be used as a therapeutic unit. Yet this would be eminently suitable. It must be evident from the description given of the mutual consideration and support the residents found in one and other that they already provide for themselves the basis of a therapeutic community.

Finally, we must return to the failure of matrons to recognize the need for casework. This must be largely due to lack of appropriate training, and the evidence of this survey argues powerfully for the need for specific training for residential care on the lines recommended by the Williams Committee. As the Committee has demonstrated, kindness and good intentions, though essential, are not enough in residential care. Staff require training to identify the particular needs of their clients and knowledge of a wide range of subjects to answer them. It is vital that they should be able to do this for unmarried mothers. The mental health of any mother and her baby is influenced by the treatment the woman receives during pregnancy and the early days of motherhood.[1] This gives those who work with unmarried mothers special opportunities and added responsibility; the quality of their care will largely determine 'whether the pregnancy will be a maturing influence or a deeply damaging one'.[2]

[1] Caplan 1961.
[2] Gough 1964.

15

ASSESSMENT AND CONCLUSIONS

The object of this study, as described in the first chapter, was to examine the policies and practices of Mother and Baby Homes in the light of present day needs. Yet it is evident that present day needs are not clearly defined or well understood, and the whole subject of illegitimacy is one in which speculation is rife and theories little tested. The Homes we visited are assessed here on the basis of the information collected during the survey, but it is recognized that this is a restricted study, and much about the problems and treatment of illegitimate maternity remains unknown. In this chapter we attempt to draw together and stress some of the considerations in the body of the report most relevant to the development of the service.

NEED FOR MOTHER AND BABY HOMES

In the introductory chapter we referred to the current questioning of the residential method of care and the emphasis in many different fields of social work on providing services within the community to prevent the necessity for care away from home. The first question to consider therefore is whether Mother and Baby Homes are really necessary.

The answer to this has to come from the social workers who interpret the needs of their clients, and from the unmarried mothers themselves, from the reasons they gave for going into a Mother and Baby Home, and from their experiences during their stay. On this evidence, Mother and Baby Homes are clearly necessary. We have noted several times the confusion in attitudes towards Mother and Baby Homes, and in particular how the expectations of social workers differ in regard to them. The residents, themselves, held conflicting opinions about the value and purpose of the Homes, but despite these differences of opinion, it is possible to see three functions for Mother and Baby Homes emerging from the present use of their facilities. These functions are similar to those recently ascribed to Children's Homes.[1]

First and most basically, Mother and Baby Homes fulfil a simple function of accommodation. There will always be some unmarried mothers for whom provision cannot be made in any other way. These women and girls are likely to be homeless, and to have problems which make the use of alternative services inappropriate. They must have somewhere to live, and because of the physical and medical care required during the weeks around the confinement period they need accommodation in a Mother and Baby Home.

The second function of Mother and Baby Homes may be described as the provision of an alternative to other types of service. Many of the unmarried mothers who are unable or unwilling to remain in their own home, or who would benefit from a period away from their families could be helped in a variety of ways; by living *au-pair* in a family, for example, or by arranging foster-care for the baby. Amongst these girls there will be some—because they are young, or because they want the comfort and companionship of being with other unmarried mothers —for whom a Mother and Baby Home may represent the most convenient or appropriate service.

Thirdly, Mother and Baby Homes may offer the best method of treatment, for it will be in the environment of the Mother and Baby that some unmarried mothers can best be helped to work through the social and emotional problems of their illegitimate maternity. In these cases, Mother and Baby Homes can be seen to fulfil a function of care.

These three functions are not entirely distinct. Each merges into the other. Even so, the distinctions serve to illustrate that Mother and Baby Homes do fulfil specific and different functions in different circumstances. When Mother and Baby Homes are viewed in this way, the conflict between community and residential care becomes unreal. As in other fields, it is seen that the needs for the different types of services exist independently of one another, and that residential provision and community care are complementary. Indeed if Mother and Baby Homes are to serve the functions listed above, it can be argued that they will be used to their best advantage only when good alternative services are available.

ADEQUACY OF THE SERVICE

It is usual to assess a service in terms of its objectives. This cannot be done for Mother and Baby Homes. Their aims are neither clearly

[1] Huws Jones 1966.

stated nor even tacitly agreed. Because of this, they are considered here on the basis of the functions outlined above. We have however limited the discussion to the two functions of 'accommodation' and 'care'. The function of Mother and Baby Homes as the most convenient of several alternative services is not considered further, partly because when the Homes are used in this way they may be required to provide little more than 'accommodation' or almost as much as 'care', and partly because this function can only be properly assessed in relation to the quality and availability of other alternative services.

The Function of Accommodation
By their very nature, all residential institutions provide accommodation. However, the quality of facilities accepted as adequate will vary according to whether the institution in question is a five star hotel or a temporary lodging house. Perhaps a fair standard by which to judge the adequacy of accommodation in Mother and Baby Homes would be that of a hostel or boarding house. When the material standards of the Mother and Baby Homes were assessed on this basis, the standards of the best Home far surpassed what might be expected; in most however, the shabbiness, discomfort and adequacy of the provision was far below that which would be considered tolerable. Similarly, the status of the residents in a Mother and Baby Home compares unfavourably with that of the residents in the institutions chosen for comparison. For the unmarried mothers, the rules, the restrictions, the invasion of privacy and the erosion of responsibility were far in excess of any limitations on personal freedom a resident in a hostel or boarding house might have to accept.

The period for which accommodation is available is relevant in this context. The policy towards length of stay will be discussed later in relation to the function of 'care', but even if Mother and Baby Homes aim at no more than the provision of accommodation the prevalent practice of fixing the length of stay is difficult to justify. During our visits we were frequently told of the financial necessity to keep the Homes full; this was held to be administratively impossible unless the period of stay was fixed. The survey produced little evidence to support this theory. There were empty beds in all but four of the Homes visited and altogether one-sixth of the total number of beds were unoccupied. By contrast, four Homes had more than their quota of residents, and one of these which the matron described as 'permanently over-full' had no fixed ruling on the length of stay. The policy of providing accommodation as and when necessary may give rise to administrative difficulties. They cannot be insurmountable; the seven Homes with no fixed length of stay demonstrated that a flexible policy is practicable. It should be recognized that a fixed length of stay means forcing accommodation on some residents when they do not want it, and excluding others when they do. If financial considerations are the only obstacle to an indeterminate length of stay, the Homes should raise their fees to allow for a proportion of beds to be unoccupied at any one time.

The Function of Care

Judging by the Homes we visited, this is the function which Mother and Baby Homes are at present least likely to fulfil. Yet it is also the function through which they could achieve most. By examining both the best and the worst aspects of the Homes visited, it is possible to see the potential for a service of care and the barriers which prevent its fulfilment.

The potential for a service of care exists in the comfort and support which the residents find in the Homes. Perhaps the most striking aspect of this research was the degree of support the residents were able to find in each other. The comfort of being together, their conscious efforts to help one another, and their tolerance of outbursts of temperament have all been mentioned, but the benefits of this mutual support cannot be overstressed.

Then there was the support the residents received from the staff. The good relationships that could be achieved have been instanced, but two other points require a mention. The simple fact that the staff are in the Mother and Baby Home before the residents arrive, and will still be there after they leave, is in itself a help; the staff have seen so many unmarried mothers in the same position, going through the same problems, and this lessens what each unmarried mother tends to see as her own unique and insurmountable unhappiness. The staff also help to alleviate the residents' feelings of social rejection. Unmarried mothers suffer keenly from a sense of social ostracism,[1] and the natural acceptance of non-condemning adults, such as the staff provide, can be a real help towards overcoming it.

Allied with this last point is the asylum function which the Homes fulfil. The residents see the Homes as a safe shelter from a hostile environment; 'a real haven of peace' was one description. That this function should be so important may seem surprising. Matrons and social workers told us repeatedly of the change in social attitudes to

[1] *Bulletin* 1966.

the unmarried mother that has taken place over the last twenty or thirty years. Now, it is said there is far more tolerance of the unmarried mother; she is no longer the outcast that she was. Although this may be true, the same period has seen the increasing readiness of society to accept all forms of deviant behaviour. The unmarried mother has shared in a general widening of sympathy, but it must be doubted whether her relative position on the scale of public tolerance has improved at all. There can be few groups who continue to suffer so much condemnation and receive so little help. The poor material standards in Mother and Baby Homes, the crippling financial problems, and the inadequate statutory supervision of the service, all testify to this. So, too, does the fact that any evidence of concern for unmarried mothers can still be branded as an encouragement to promiscuity.[1]

We now turn to the worst aspects of the Homes visited. First, despite the good staff-resident relationships noted in some Homes, there was the general lack of social work support demonstrated particularly by the last chapter. With a few exceptions neither matrons nor outdoor workers answered the residents' evident need for a supportive relationship. For the residents of Mother and Baby Homes, practical help and kindness is not enough. Nor is it sufficient to receive a general assurance of the matron's or social worker's readiness to assist with any problem. If the residents themselves are only half aware of the more subtle problems of their situation, a more active approach is necessary. Matrons and social workers must have the skill and sensitivity to recognize the need for support even when there is no direct request for it. They must have the ability to draw out a client's difficulties, and to help her to formulate and face up to her own problems. This kind of support is essential to a service of care. The inadequacy of the help at present provided is all the more serious in view of theories blaming the failure to resolve emotional conflicts underlying a pregnancy for repeated illegitimate maternities, and the perpetuation of the problem from one generation to another. Recent research in America also suggests that prolonged maternal anxieties and emotional stress during pregnancy may have adverse effects on the development of the foetus leading to difficulties of adaption in the newborn baby,[2] and this is an added argument for casework help during pregnancy. Although these theories are still somewhat speculative, in terms of community mental health the importance of the problems they seek to explain is incalculable.

[1] N.C.U.M.C. 1964 Memorandum to Lord Longford's Study Group on Penal Reform.
[2] See Mussen, Conger, and Kagan 1963.

Secondly, there is the 'mothering situation'. It has been suggested that this needs to be reviewed in many Homes, and it may be that the mothering situation will differ according to whether Homes interpret their purpose as one of accommodation or care. While a service of accommodation would be expected to do no more than house the mother and child for a temporary period, a service of care might use the mothering situation as a means of assisting a mother to work through her difficulties. In either case we face the need for a better knowledge and understanding of the problems and needs of ambiguous maternity.

Finally, we must return to the controversial question of a fixed length of stay. The main arguments against a flexible policy are those of administrative convenience, and in a service of care such arguments cannot be allowed to take precedence over individual needs. Though there is a need for flexibility both before and after the baby's birth, it is the insistence on a post-natal stay and the customary fixing of this at a minimum of six weeks, even for mothers who are surrendering their child for adoption, which causes the greatest concern, and this deserves special attention. The justification for requiring a post-natal stay was based on the theory that the long term interests of both mother and child demand that they should spend some time together. This is one of the many untested theories concerning illegitimacy. The question of whether or not an unmarried mother should care for or even see her child when he is to be placed for adoption is bitterly contested amongst all those concerned with the care of unmarried mothers and illegitimate children.[1] Some believe emphatically that unmarried mothers should be allowed to fulfil their motherhood, and that there is great benefit for both mother and child in being together for a short time. Others hold equally firmly that it brings no gain to the baby and can only cause suffering to the mother. A third view maintains that the interests of mother and child conflict. Similar divergent views were expressed by the unmarried mothers themselves.[2] The plain fact of the matter is that we do not know how either the unmarried mother or her baby is affected by being together or apart during these few weeks; within the present state of knowledge, there are no grounds for forcing a post-natal stay on an unwilling mother.

There is even less justification for fixing a particular number of weeks as a minimum period of stay. Even amongst residents who felt

---

[1] This question is discussed in an article on 'Adoption and the Natural Mother' Yelloly, 1965.
[2] cf Greenland 1958.

that a post-natal stay was usually helpful there was general agreement that six weeks was too long. One matron who also believed that a short time with the baby was advisable felt that the present period imposed too great a strain on the mothers. This factor is of special importance in cases where an adoption cannot be made within the normal six week period. The residents in one Home had been shocked to see the effect on a mother of an adoption delayed until three months; 'You could see her ageing,' they said. 'It turned her into an old woman.' Further consideration of the best practice in such cases is very necessary.

CONCLUSIONS

Of the five themes identified in the first chapter as forming the context of the work of Mother and Baby Homes, the one that dominates this report is the uncertain purpose of the Home. This uncertainty must be resolved if the service is to develop. As we have suggested the original purpose of reform is no longer generally accepted and the choice for the future would seem to lie between offering a service of accommodation or one of residential care. If the Homes choose the latter alternative then certain fundamental issues must be considered.

In the first place the Homes must exploit the therapeutic value of relationships formed within the Home, in particular making the maximum use of the mutual support generated by the group of residents. Consideration should be given to ways in which the group can be used to help residents through the emotional difficulties of their period in the Home, and to support them in planning for the future. This will mean helping some to become reconciled to parting with their child, while building up the confidence of others in their capacity to be a mother. We need to know how far the needs of these different groups are compatible. Do the charges of selfishness, for example, levelled by the other residents at the mothers who are planning to keep their baby undermine the confidence of these girls in their decision? Should the mothers who are keeping their children be treated separately from those who are placing the baby for adoption? Or does the presence of unmarried mothers from both groups together help each towards a more realistic assessment of their decision and its consequences?

If the supportive role of the group is to be exploited, then the factors making for group cohesion must also be studied. The size of the Home has been mentioned as an influence on relationships. Admission criteria is another relevant factor, and it is doubtful how far some of the existing criteria such as religious denomination, place of residence, number of previous pregnancies or marital status, either help or hinder the formation of a congenial group. Age would appear to be a useful criterion and we have suggested that further use could be made of this as a selective factor. The whole basis of admission policy needs to be reviewed and it is possible that quite different systems of classification might prove appropriate; one based for example on the severity of a client's problems, so that the service of residential care would range through various forms of accommodation, from facilities with minimal support and supervision, to Homes providing intensive casework and psychiatric care. Alternatively, if it should prove practicable to help the majority of unmarried mothers to a decision about their baby during pregnancy, this would raise the possibility of providing special facilities for mothers who definitely intend to keep their babies, as is done for example, in Italy.[1]

If Mother and Baby Homes are to offer a service of care, they must be adequately staffed and adequately financed. Staffing establishments must be realistic, and staff should have specific training in residential care when this becomes available. Organizations providing Homes must have the financial resources to employ the necessary staff, to maintain the building in good order, to enable staff and residents to live in a reasonable degree of comfort, and to permit a flexible policy on length of stay. If necessary the Homes must raise their fees in order to do these things. In the context of finance the system of local authority grant aid for residential care should be rationalized. Considerable administrative inconvenience is caused by the complexity and discrepancies of present practices and it is highly unsatisfactory that despite possible help from Social Security Benefits and, in some instances, from the children's department, some unmarried mothers are still unable to raise the full fees for a Mother and Baby Home.

The present structure of the service needs re-examination. If a service of care is to be implemented, co-ordination of existing facilities is essential, particularly if individual Homes are to be more selective in their intake. The present statutory framework of the service also needs revision for it fails to ensure the provision of adequate standards.

In the first place some general system of registration applicable to all Mother and Baby Homes is essential. It is known that most of the voluntary organizations would welcome registration,[2] and without it

[1] The work of the 'Villaggio della Madre e del Faneiullo' in Milan was described in a paper read to the First International Congress of Psychiatry, 1964, by Elda Scarzella Mazzocchi.
[2] Memorandum submitted by the N.C.U.M.C. to Williams Committee 1964.

any overall improvement in the standard of service is unlikely. At present registration as a Nursing Home is the only form of registration open to Mother and Baby Homes. But Mother and Baby Homes are not Nursing Homes; the service they provide differs from that of a Nursing Home in many respects. A new and more suitable form of registration is required.

Secondly the present system of inspection must be changed. Local health authority inspection is clearly unsatisfactory. Only four Homes visited were not officially inspected, yet conditions in many were far from adequate. One of the worst voluntary Homes had been inspected regularly for years. The matron said frankly that she saw no value in local authority supervision if such low standards continued to be tolerated, and it is relevant in this context that Homes run directly by local authorities were not always amongst the best. On the evidence of this survey, it would seem that existing local health authorities are too small to be the units of supervision. The residential care of unmarried mothers is itself a very small service. To establish a good standard of care the inspecting authority must be able to draw on a broad fund of knowledge and comparative experience. This can only be achieved through inspection on a national basis.

In considering the development of Mother and Baby Homes, it is necessary again to refer to the other services used by unmarried mothers. If Mother and Baby Homes are to provide the type of service envisaged here, they cannot develop in isolation. They must form part of a range of services which will include facilities such as fostering, nursery care and the provision of grants, allowances and subsidized lodging schemes. There must be greater integration between existing residential and community provision and closer co-operation between the staff of the different services. Mother and Baby Homes must not be used indiscriminately for any unmarried mother requiring help around the confinement period. They should be regarded primarily as a specialist service for those with a real need for residential care.

Finally, we have to return to the social setting of work with unmarried mothers, and to the ambivalent attitude of society towards them. The type and quality of any social service largely reflects the attitude of the community to the group for which provision is being made. For this reason change and development in a service is partly dependent on community agreement. This survey has demonstrated the need for a service of care, and we have argued that such a service would make a positive contribution to community mental health. We have stressed repeatedly that the Homes must decide their purpose.

But whether they should accept a purpose of care is not entirely a decision for the Homes alone. It is also a choice facing society. Ultimately, the community must decide what it wants Mother and Baby Homes to do; for the community has to provide the means—the money, the staff and the knowledge—for the Homes to fulfil their purpose.

RESEARCH MATERIAL

List of information available for consultation at the National Council for the Unmarried Mother and Her Child, 255 Kentish Town Road, London, N.W.5, and at the National Institute for Social Work Training, Mary Ward House, Tavistock Place, London, W.C.1. Duplicated sets of the information may be purchased from the National Council for the Unmarried Mother and Her Child.

Questionnaires and lists of topics for discussion during interviews.

    (a) Matrons.   (b) Residents.   (c) Social Workers.

Tables.
- (a) *Residents*.
    1. Marital Status.
    2. Number of other children.
    3. Nationality.
    4. Age: (a) by each year; (b) by 5 yr. age-groups.
    5. Family background: (a) summary of family structure: (b) details.
    6. Mother's knowledge about the baby: (a) whether she knew; (b) when she got to know.
    7. Father's knowledge about the baby: (a) whether he knew; (b) when he got to know.
    8. Number of residents who had moved during pregnancy.
    9. Residents' town in relation to parents' town at time of conception.
    10. Residents' town in relation to parents' town before entering Home.
    11. Decision about the baby: (a) total sample; (b) expectant mothers by each region; (c) mothers by each region; (d) by age group.
    12. Plans for care of baby of 40 residents keeping their child.
    13. Stage of pregnancy when residents first consulted a doctor about the pregnancy.
    14. Time of starting regular ante-natal care.
    15. Jobs: (a) last occupation before coming into the Home (all residents); (b) change of occupation during pregnancy; (c) stage of pregnancy at which residents gave up work.
    16. Contact with putative father while in Mother and Baby Home, by age of residents.
    17. Residents' reasons for coming into a Mother and Baby Home.

(b) *Social Workers.*
   1. Number of social workers with whom residents had been in touch.
   2. Kind of social worker with whom resident had first made contact.
   3. Source of contact for first social worker.
   4. Number of residents no longer in touch with first worker, by kind of worker first contacted.
   5. Kind of social worker with whom residents were in touch at time of interview.
   6. Time of contact with social workers: (a) all residents: contact with first worker; (b) residents who had been in touch with more than one worker: time of contacting 1st and present workers.
   7. Number of meetings with social workers before admission to Mother and Baby Home analysed by stage of pregnancy at which contact was first made; (a) residents who had been in touch with only one worker; (b) residents who had been in touch with more than one worker: (i) amount of contact with first worker; (ii) amount of contact with present worker.
   8. Number of times residents were visited by social workers during their stay.
   9. Length of time residents unvisited by a social worker had been in Home.

(c) *Staff.*
   1. Staff establishment in each Home showing size of Home, number, function, and qualifications of resident and non-resident staff employed, official vacancies, and matrons' views of sufficiency of full establishment.
   2. Summary of staff qualifications.

Summary of information supplied by Medical Officers of Health regarding the policy and practice of their Authority, towards unmarried mothers in need of residential accommodation and towards voluntary organizations providing services for unmarried mothers.
   1. Aid to unmarried mothers in need of residential accommodation;
   2. Grants to Mother and Baby Homes and Moral Welfare Organizations;
   3. Registration of Mother and Baby Homes by Local Health Authorities.

BIBLIOGRAPHY AND LIST OF REFERENCES
(*=publication not referred to in the text)

ANDERSON, E. W., KENNA, J. C. and HAMILTON, M. W.
  (1960) 'A Study of Extra-Marital Conception in Adolescence', *Psychiatria et Neurologia*, Vol. 139, No. 6.

BALL, PATRICIA
  (1962) 'A Study of Extra-Marital Pregnancy: based on 100 Social Case Histories', unpublished thesis presented in the University of Liverpool.

*BRANSBY, E. R. and ELLIOT, RACHEL A.
  (1959) 'The Unmarried Mother and Her Child', monthly *Bulletin* of the Ministry of Health, Vol. 18.

Board for Social Responsibility of the National Assembly of the Church of England.
  (1964–7) *Directories of Church of England Moral Welfare Work*.
  (1966) 'Fatherless by Law'.

BOWLBY, J.
  (1951) *Maternal Care & Mental Health*, W.H.O.

(The) *Bulletin* of the Moral Welfare Workers Association
  (1966) 'The Client's Need for Residential Accommodation', Vol. 4, No. 2.

CAPLAN, GERALD
  (1961) *An Approach to Community Mental Health*, Tavistock.

Catholic Child Welfare Council
  Directory of Children's Homes in England and Wales.

CHAMBERLAIN, ROMA N.
  (1959) 'A Study of Natural Childbirth', Monthly *Bulletin* of the Ministry of Health, Vol. 18.

FERGUSON, S. M. and FITZGERALD, H.
  (1954) *Studies in the Social Services*. H.M.S.O.

*GARRARD, JESSIE
  (1967) 'Illegitimacy', *The Practitioner*, No. 1184, Vol. 198.

GOODACRE, IRIS
  (1966) *Adoption Policy and Practice*. National Institute for Social Work Training, Series No. 9, Allen & Unwin.

GOUGH, DONALD
  (1961) 'Work with Unmarried Mothers', *The Almoner*, Vol. 13, No. 12.
  (1966) *Understanding Unmarried Mothers: Observations by a Psychoanalyst*, N.C.U.M.C.

GREENLAND, CYRIL
- (1957) 'Unmarried Parenthood: Ecological Aspects', *The Lancet*.
- (1958) 'The Unmarried Mother and Her Child', *Child Care*: The Quarterly Review of the National Council of Associated Children's Homes, Vol. 12, No. 3.

HALL, PENELOPE M. and HOWES, ISMENE V.
- (1965) *The Church in Social Work*. Routledge & Kegan Paul.

HUWS JONES, ROBIN
- (1966) 'The Staffing of Residential Homes', paper presented to the 17th Annual Conference of the Association of Children's Officers 1966, published in *The Child in Care*: Journal of the Residential Child Care Association.

HYTTEN, F. E.
- (1957) 'Can Every Mother Breast Feed her Baby?', An account of a lactation study in Aberdeen. *Nursing Mirror*, 31 May.

HYTTEN, F. E., YORSTON, JESSIE C. and THOMSON, A. M.
- (1958) 'Difficulties associated with breast-feeding', *British Medical Journal*, 8 February, Vol. i.

JACOBS, J.
- (1964) 'Illegitimacy, Adoption and the Care-giving Professionals', *International Journal of Social Psychiatry*. Special Edition No. 3.

JONES, KATHLEEN
- (1966) *The Compassionate Society*. S.P.C.K.

*MADDISON, ARTHUR J. S.
- (1914) *Hints on Rescue Work*. Reformatory and Refuge Union.

MEYER, H. J., JONES, W. and BORGATTA, E. F.
- (1956) 'The Decision of Unmarried Mothers to Keep or Surrender their Babies', *Social Work* (Journal of the National Association of Social Workers) Vol. 1, No. 2.

MILLER, DEREK
- (1964) *Growth to Freedom*. Tavistock.

MUSSEN, PAUL H., CONGER, JOHN J and KAGAN, JEROME
- (1963) *Child Development and Personality*. 2nd edition. Harper and Row.

Ministry of Health
- (1943) *Circular 2866
- (1947) *Circular 118/47
- (1963) *Circular 18/63
- (1958) Unpublished Study of Mother and Baby Homes.
- (1965) 'Enquiry into sudden death in Infancy', *Reports on Public Health and Medical Subjects*, No. 113. H.M.S.O.

National Council for the Unmarried Mother and Her Child,
Memoranda:
- (1963) 'A project concerning residential care for the unmarried mother and her child,'

(1964) 'Staffing in Residential Homes and Institutions', a memorandum submitted to the Williams Committee.
(1964) 'Social Provision for the illegitimate child and his mother', a memorandum submitted to Lord Longford's Study Group on Penal Reform.
Conference Proceedings:
(1964) *'The Unmarried Mother and Her Child in Residential Care'
(1964) *'Fatherless Families'—Conference organized jointly by N.C.U.M.C. and Council for Children's Welfare
(1966) 'Pregnancy in Adolescence'
Other Publications:
(1964) 'Standards in Mother and Baby Homes'—Leaflet 1, 'Material Standards'.
(1967) 'Standards in Mother and Baby Homes'—Leaflet 2 'Diet and Catering'.
(1964) **Legal Aspects of Illegitimacy*, G. S. Wilkinson.
(1964) *Directory of Homes and Hostels for the Care of Unmarried Mothers and their Children.*

*PINCHBECK, IVY
(1954) 'Social Attitudes towards Illegitimacy', *British Journal of Sociology*, Vol. 5.

Political and Economic Planning,
(1946) 'The Unmarried Mother', *Planning*, No. 255.

Registrar General
(1964) *Statistical Review of England and Wales*, Part II, H.M.S.O.

Report of the Maternity Services Committee (Cranbrooke)
(1959) Ministry of Health, H.M.S.O.

*'Report of the Working Party on Social Workers in the Local Authority Health and Welfare Services' (Younghusband),
(1959) Ministry of Health, H.M.S.O.

Report of a Committee of Enquiry set up by the National Council of Social Service (Williams),
(1967) *Caring for People*, National Institute for Social Work Training Series, No. 11, Allen & Unwin.

Salvation Army *Yearbook* (1964)

SPICER, C. C. and LIPWORTH, L.
(1966) 'Regional and Social Factors in Infant Mortality', General Register Office, *Studies on Medical & Population Subjects*, No. 19, H.M.S.O.

TILLEY, MARGARET
(1965) 'Moral Welfare', published in *Trends in Social Welfare*, edited by James Farndale, Westminster Series, Pergamon Press.

THOMPSON, BARBARA
(1956) 'Social Study of Illegitimate Maternities', *British Journal of Preventive and Social Medicine*.

TOWNSEND, PETER
(1962) *The Last Refuge*. Routledge & Kegan Paul.
*TRENHOLME, EDWARD C.
(1927) *Rescue Work*. S.P.C.K.
*WIMPERIS, VIRGINIA
(1960) *The Unmarried Mother and Her Child*. Allen & Unwin.
*WYNN, MARGARET
(1964) *Fatherless Families*. Michael Joseph.
YELLOLY, MARGARET A.
(1964) 'Social Casework with Unmarried Parents: A Critical evaluation of its Theoretical Aspects in the light of a study of Extra-Marital Pregnancies', unpublished thesis presented for the degree of M.A. in the University of Liverpool.
(1965) 'Factors relating to an adoption decision by the mothers of illegitimate infants'. *Sociological Review*, Vol. 13, No. 1.
(1966) 'Adoption and the Natural Mother'. *Case Conference*, Vol. 13, No. 8.
YOUNG, LEONTINE
(1954) *Out of Wedlock*. McGraw-Hill.

Acts, England and Wales
1. Children Act 1948
2. Children and Young Persons Act 1963
3. Legitimacy Act 1959
4. National Assistance Act 1946
5. National Health Service Act 1946
6. Nursing Homes Act 1963
7. Public Health Act 1936